GRIDLOCK NATION

KWASI KWARTENG AND JONATHAN DUPONT

GRIDLOCK NATION

Why Britain's transport systems are heading towards gridlock and what we can do to stop it

Biteback Publishing

First published in Great Britain in 2011 by
Biteback Publishing Ltd
Westminster Tower
3 Albert Embankment
London
SE1 7SP

ISBN 978-1-84954-112-1

10 9 8 7 6 5 4 3 2 1

A CIP catalogue record for this book is available from the
British Library.

Set in Sabon and Helvetica Neue by Namkwan Cho
Cover design by Namkwan Cho

Printed and bound in Great Britain by
CPI Cox & Wyman, Reading, RG1 8EX

CONTENTS

ACKNOWLEDGEMENTS

This book would not have been possible without the ideas of many people who have thought and written about transport in the past. We would like to express our gratitude to all those who gave their time in discussing the subject. A special thanks is dedicated to Bridget Rosewell who generously read an earlier draft. Thanks are also due to Sarah Fitch who provided a great deal of administrative help. Our research was greatly assisted by staff at the National Archives in Kew and at the Library of the House of Commons. Finally, we would like to acknowledge Iain Dale for his support and enthusiasm for the project from the very beginning, and Sam Carter for his commitment to publish the book in a timely manner. Their team at Biteback have all been wonderfully supportive.

INTRODUCTION

What will British transport look like fifty years from today?

Half neglected for decades, the roads between our major cities are full. Within towns and cities, traffic is lucky to move at all. Traffic jams frequently last for days on end.

Trains are little better. Passengers complain of fare increases year on year, despite never being able to find a seat. Commuters are shoved into packed Tube carriages by white-gloved attendants.

Weary travellers shuffle off their plane past endless rows of duty free shops, before security finally allows them to take a train home. It has become too expensive for all but the seriously wealthy to fly.

But worse than the everyday inconveniences are the wider effects on the rest of the country. Foreign companies flee London, unwilling to stay in a city so cut off from the world economy. Manufacturing firms go bust, unable to receive inputs or send goods out from their factory. The price of imported goods climbs. Because so many polluting cars are trapped in traffic, our carbon emissions soar.

Is this just a dark fantasy, or is a Gridlock Nation the inevitable result of today's transport policy?

For the last fifty years, the shape of our transport systems has remained roughly the same. We take a car, the bus or tube to get to work; motorways or trains to move between cities; jumbo jets to fly overseas.

But in the coming decades our transport systems will have to adapt to unprecedented challenges. The threat of climate change means we have to end our transport's current reliance on fossil fuels. An increasing population

will gridlock our economy unless we solve today's congestion problems. In short, we'll need a complete transforma-
tion of the way transport works.

Even if the coming challenges didn't exist, few today
would cite Britain's transport as a source of pride. Transport
is almost as popular a source of British grumbling as
the weather.

This is a book for anyone who has wondered why our
roads are so crowded or railways so expensive. Why, when
in most of one's life the amount of time spent queuing is
going down, is the time we must spend in traffic jams going
up? Why do rail fares continue to rise year after year – even
as the government keeps handing additional subsidy to
Network Rail? Why do airports seem more concerned with
shops than passenger comfort? Are all the restrictions on
what we take on the plane really making us safer? How can
the Chinese build a couple of airports and a high speed rail
network in the time it takes for us to add a single terminal?

The good news is that many of these issues can be
solved, using nothing more than ordinary economics and a
little bit of common sense. During the course of this book,
we'll see how we can make our roads flow freely again, stop
pouring so much money into our railways, and make flying
a pleasure again.

Unfortunately, many other answers to our problems will
depend as much on new technology as new policy.

The Future of Transport?

As we grow up, our stories are filled by futuristic science
fiction methods of transport from movies and television.
We see the *Starship Enterprise* proudly navigating the stars,
or the *Millennium Falcon* dodging enemy attacks.

The 1950s were full of such scientific visions: flying cars,
nuclear powered trains and supersonic jet liners. But these
visions were not just the wild fantasises of writers, rather
the confident predictions of transport companies themselves.

In 1958, Ford designed a concept car, the *Nucleon*, which was planned to run 5,000 miles on a single atomic battery. The Santa Fe railroad ran magazine ads promising fission reactor trains within twenty years.[1]

In 1940, General Motors sponsored an exhibition showing their prediction for roads in the 1960s: cars driving themselves on motorways that could cross the American continent in twenty-four hours.[2] The motorways were to come to pass. The driverless cars were not.

But was it so unreasonable to hope for such progress?

Previous science fiction visions had come true: from Jules Verne's 1870 *Nautilus* submarine through Tintin's 1953 rocket, taking him up to the stars.

Why should envisioning flying cars be any sillier than predicting talking computers, personal communicators or genetic engineering?

If not flying cars, we might have hoped to see other advances in technology. For whatever reason, progress has largely stood still since the 1950s. We use the same basic forms of vehicles sixty years later as we did then.

Compare this to the experience of a typical Victorian. Florence Nightingale was born in 1820 and died in 1910. Across her lifetime she saw the world transformed: a vast network of steam railways crossing continents and enabling an ordinary man to travel faster than a horse's gallop for the first time; steam turbine powered ships, no longer constrained by the randomness of wind or tide; a second transport revolution, as the internal combustion engine removed the need for horses altogether; the construction of an electric railway deep underground; and even the Wright brothers' first heavier-than-air flight.

Ever since, progress seems to have stalled. We've tinkered at the edges of technology, making our vehicles safer and

---

1   http://chronopause.com/index.php/2011/02/07/67/
2   O'Toole, 2009, p. 191

more comfortable – but there have been no real advances to change our lifestyle. The rocket age appears to have been a dead end. We still drive more or less the same type of cars. The first High Speed Rail appeared in 1964 in Tokyo, but the technology has spread only slowly. Our planes haven't noticeably moved on from the Boeing 747, first introduced in 1970.

Nowhere has this slowdown been starker than in Britain. In the past, Britain had an enviable record in transport innovation, from Stephenson's development of the steam railway to Frank Whittle's jet engine. The world used to come to Britain to watch and learn, while British engineers in turn crossed the globe to build its infrastructure.

In order to meet the challenges of climate change and congestion, we will need completely different types of transport. We will have to rip up the networks that have served us since the 1950s and start again.

In other words, we won't meet these challenges unless we can rediscover the technological and entrepreneurial innovation that seems to have gone missing. Small, marginal changes won't get us where we need to go.

There is, however, some good news. Across the world we're beginning to see the faint beginnings of just such a revolution. Innovators and developers are working on exciting-sounding technologies from self driving cars to carbon free planes. This is no longer science fiction, but cutting edge research, happening today.

But that doesn't mean progress is inevitable. Much of today's transport debate is still confused by myths that stop us from the necessary debate on the best way forward.

The Myths in Transport
For all the protests and attacks it receives from politicians, it simply isn't true that aviation is the worst threat faced by the environment. Railway privatisation didn't compromise safety. Building new roads doesn't always lead to more traffic filling them.

But then, these myths haven't entirely been confined to one side of the partisan debate either. British aviation is not doomed without the creation of third runway. Historically, the government has in many ways unfairly favoured the roads over railways. The creation of a new road pricing system isn't necessarily a new assault in the so-called 'war on the motorist'.

The myths that exist in transport have led to strange alliances. Tory backbenchers working alongside deep green environmentalists to stop the expansion of Britain's premier airport; a Conservative Mayor blocking the further introduction of market reforms on Britain's state run roads; a Labour Party pumping subsidy into private companies and the railways.

But most of all these myths have made it hard to look again at the transport system on a rational, pragmatic basis. Transport need not be political. Turning the debate into an acrimonious partisan war helps nobody, whether they are businessmen or environmentalists, drivers or passengers.

Indeed, transport has long had its civil war. On one side are those in favour of public transport, compact cities and strict limits on aviation. On the other, there are those who complain bitterly of the war against the driver, and the vast amounts of money poured into inherently unviable railways.

Neither side is fully right or, for that matter, fully wrong in their accusations – but the false dividing lines between public and private transport help nobody. To meet its future needs, Britain will indeed need more railways and cycle lanes, but more roads and airports as well.

The biggest myth of all, however, is that transport only prospers when planned effectively by government bureaucrats.

In many ways, transport has always been trapped in the middle of the ideological war between left and right. Should it be just another private product like a newspaper or supermarket, or a public service like health and education? Across the course of the twentieth century transport has fluctuated between the two like few other areas of our economy. This has left a legacy of confused thinking and stale arguments.

This book comes down firmly on the former side of the argument: transport is essential to our society, but there is nothing in particular about it that makes it fundamentally different from other areas of our economy. Nevertheless, transport is one of the few areas of public life in which people continue to argue in favour of government control and Stalinist-style long-term planning. Most long-term decisions on transport infrastructure are determined by well-meaning bureaucrats, relying on detailed projections of traffic demand up to thirty years in the future.

But transport isn't any more complex or essential than other fundamental areas of our economy, such as food, clothes, the media or energy. Many such companies are enormously complex, requiring the co-ordination of thousands of people and supply chains spreading across the world. Without any one of these products our life would be significantly worse off – and yet, for the most part, we trust in well regulated free markets to provide these services for us.

As we'll see, the failure of 'Planners' has left a legacy of congestion, expensive prices and misery for travellers.

We don't need new thinking in the transport system – we just need to make use of the same mainstream, common sense ideas which work for the rest of our economy.

We need more trial and error, more experimentation and bold new ideas. The only way to get that is to free transport from the planning and regulation that currently hold it back.

When possible, we should let individuals make their own choices, as long as they're prepared to pay the full costs their choices impose on others. Rather than ration excess demand with long queues for limited road space or airport slots, we should look into what benefits can be derived from prices and markets. At the same time, private companies shouldn't be able to take advantage of public funds, earning risk free profits off government contracts.

Following these principles, we shall see why our roads are so full, why Heathrow is packed with shops and what exactly went wrong in the railways. We shall look at how transport can do its part to tackle climate change, and examine how that can be reconciled with the infrastructure needed to support the country's growth.

We'll explore the conflict between planners and innovators throughout history and across the world. We'll look back at the Romans' problems with traffic jams and the Georgian war against the driver. We'll take in the strange science fiction dreams of Victorian engineers and the cutthroat competition of American rail barons. We'll see what we can learn from past solutions that have been attempted throughout history, from Britain's original attempt at road pricing to the successes (and failures) of the grand nationalisation experiment.

And finally we'll look at what might come next: a private sector revolution in space, creating the world's first space tourists; battery powered vehicles, driving themselves to pick up your relatives from the station; an end to the traditional car, and the many vehicles that might replace it.

If we learn the right lessons, then Britain can indeed avoid becoming a Gridlock Nation.

PART ONE

HOW WE GOT HERE

THE HISTORY OF TRANSPORT

It's Monday morning. You wake up, a little hung over from the weekend's excesses, the rising sun acting as your alarm clock.

You walk from your cramped and dirty village home to the field where your crops grow, and begin your day's long, back breaking work.

This is your routine, day after day, week after week. You've never travelled much more than a few miles from your home, although the horse-drawn carriages that clatter past occasionally bring news from the big city.

This could be the typical day of your average worker in the late eighteenth century – but then it could be your typical day for the average worker in the late eighth century as well.

Aside from fluctuations in population, there was little change in ordinary life for normal people ever since the invention of farming, many thousands of years ago. Fundamentally the range of human movement was limited by the restrictions of the boat and the horse.

In scarcely more than a couple of generations in the nineteenth century, by contrast, everything about this picture would have changed.

When we think of the acceleration in economic growth of the nineteenth century we think of the factory and its smoking chimneys. Nevertheless, the fundamental changes to our society were as much about transport revolution as industrial revolution. The steam train, more reliable shipping and later, internal combustion, changed the world.

This transport revolution radically dropped the cost of trade and grew the economy. It brought the country and world closer together, acting as the most important change in communications since the invention of the printing press. It changed the balance of military power, and brought new countries and empires together. It unleashed freedom and opportunity, in particular for the poor and vulnerable, but created new dangers through early accidents while technologies were perfected.

But there is a third part to this story, for this revolutionary speed of change has not lasted. Now, it seems, progress has slowed to a halt once more. At the same time, the twentieth century has seen a widespread government attempt to take control of transport. Only at the end of the century has it grudgingly returned a part of its power.

Has the rise of planning killed the transport revolution?

Transport before Steam

The state of transport before the nineteenth century revolution was remarkably consistent. Sails or animal muscle were used as the source of power, while the nations and empires that could control trade routes rapidly became rich. Innovation was glacially slow. Governments struggled to maintain good roads and avoid congestion in crowded city centres.

Beyond the purposes of war, transport has always had two primary functions: to move people from place to place, or to move goods from a place to them. While both can share the same vehicle, for reasons of cost as much as technology they have often followed very different paths. Goods take up far more space to transport than people, but will put up with less speed and comfort.

Mastery of new modes of transport lay behind the success of past empires. In the Ancient World power increasingly flowed towards coastal nations such as Greece as new ships helped to conquer the Mediterranean. The Romans and their famous roads could control a whole continent. Much of the explanation for the rise of the Arab nations in the seventh and eighth centuries AD lies in their mastery of the humble camel, the 'ship of the desert', giving them a crucial advantage over seafarers. The Royal Navy allowed Britain to project power across the globe and establish the most powerful Empire the world has ever seen.

Trade, or the transport of goods for freight, is probably as old as civilisation. There is evidence that ancient humans, not long after the invention of language, wore jewellery and used weapons that had travelled distances far greater than their new owners could expect to journey in a lifetime.[3] Pack animals were first domesticated around ten thousand years ago, and wheels appeared only five thousand years later in Russia.[4]

Throughout history, merchants expanded their range over longer distances across the oceans or along the world's trade routes. Control of those routes was important for the world's powers. They contributed significant tax revenues and allowed the easy movement of armies or communication of orders.

Before the era of fossil fuel power, travelling by water was by far the best way to harness the two power sources that did exist: the force of wind at open sea, and the muscle power of horse or ox.

In Britain the coasts were not only the best way to transport goods to other countries but also within its own borders. Being an island, Britain could use its coasts as the main transport artery for the majority of the goods the country needed.

Away from the coast, there was a continual process of improvement to make inland waterways more manoeuvrable. Despite the boost received from Dutch technology the process was never perfect, and Britain eventually began the construction of its own additional canal network. By the end of the eighteenth century Britain had around

3   Ridley, 2010
4   Glaesar, 2011, p. 168

two thousand miles of navigable waterway, split evenly between natural rivers, rivers that had been improved, and a completely artificially network of canals.[5]

Travelling by water cost as little as a quarter per mile as much as travelling by land,[6] and so the roads were mostly left for passengers or mail who needed the extra speed. Horse and carriage were the main means by which richer passengers could traverse the country or move around the larger cities.

This was not to stop the roads causing problems that still sound familiar today. In the millennia since Roman times the roads had been left in a poor shape, maintained as little more than mud tracks. Long journeys were far from comfortable. In theory, the network was the responsibility of the local parishes, and each citizen was under a legal obligation to spend a few days each year on their upkeep. In practice, this system proved wholly incapable of coping with the influx of new traffic from the growing Industrial Revolution.

Showing admirable reforming instincts, the government privatised the most widely used routes, handing their control over to what were known as 'turnpike trusts'. The trusts were granted a lease over the infrastructure for a fixed period of up to thirty years and in return allowed to charge passing travellers.

The turnpike trusts succeeded in improving the quality of the roads. Journey times dropped – a trip between London and Manchester that had taken four and a half days in 1754 took a mere eighteen hours by 1830.[7]

But then, the state of the roads was soon to become redundant with the coming of the railways. The horse-drawn carriages were unable to compete with steam

5   *Transport in Britain*, p. 6
6   Ibid., p. 1
7   Glaister, Burnham, Stevens, & Travers, 2006 p. 1

powered engines, and the turnpike trusts began to struggle financially. One by one they gradually passed back into public hands

A new age of transport had begun.

What Caused the Transport Revolution?
Almost since the event itself, economists and historians have debated exactly what it was that caused the economic changes that occurred in the nineteenth century. Economies that had remained more or less static since the invention of farming, the average person barely better off in 1800 than he or she might have been in 100,000 BC,[8] suddenly saw the birth of relentless, modern growth.

Some look to Britain's long record of stability and democratic, liberal institutions. Some claim that it was a record of fundamental cultural change in favour of hard work and entrepreneurialism, while others argue that Britain was fortunate in its possession of abundant deposits of coal.

The exact cause of the industrial and transport revolutions of the nineteenth century is still unclear. The best scholars can say is that it was likely some combination of favourable institutions, geography and culture – which is so vague as almost not to be saying anything at all.

What is clear is that the revolutions were not the result of progress in science alone. Although Britain, as the home of Newton and Darwin, was at the forefront of world science, it is far from clear what the exact connection is between this and later progress in technology. According to writer Matt Ridley,

> Of the four men who made the biggest advances in the steam engine – Thomas Newcomen, James Watt, Richard Trevithick and George Stephenson – three were utterly ignorant of scientific theories, and historians disagree about

---

8   Clark, 2007, p. 1

whether the fourth, Watt, derived any influence from theory at all. It was they who made possible the theories of the vacuum and the laws of thermodynamics, not vice versa.[9]

Moreover, variations of the crucial technologies that were to come together in the nineteenth century had been around for centuries. The improvement of rivers and building of canals was utilised by the very first civilisations in ancient Mesopotamia, while the use of rails was known in the classical world. The earliest system of railways we know of dates from about 600 BC, in the form of a set of stone grooves crossing the Isthmus of Corinth to avoid the dangerous sea journey around the Peloponnese.[10] The Romans seemed to make use of similar technology in their mine at Três Minas in Portugal, although the technology then seems to disappear from the Western world until the end of the Dark Ages.

When the technology reappeared, the stone grooves had been replaced by wooden rails, although their main function was still the transportation of heavy goods from mines. Gradually these early railways spread out from the mines to reach the canals, until by the seventeenth century wooden wagon ways were fairly common across the United Kingdom.

The idea of a steam engine was similarly ancient. The first plans for a simple engine were presented as far back as 75 AD by the mathematician Hero of Alexandria. Throughout history, thinkers such as Leonardo da Vinci tinkered with the idea, although it would require significantly better control of heat and vacuums before the designs could be made practical. The first significant working engines were once again developed for mines, such as Thomas Savery's 1698 'miner's friend' which was designed to pump out the water that continually seeped into the mines.

9   Ridley, 2010, p. 256
10 Lewis, 2001

Progress often depends just as much on the choices made by a society as its level of science. The first hot air balloons were flown by the Montgolfier brothers in the 1780s, but there seems to be absolutely nothing about the technology out of reach of the Romans and the advanced canvas technology they demonstrated in the roof of their circus.[11]

For whatever reason, private scientists and entrepreneurs quickly launched one new innovation after another, perfecting innovations such as steam and electricity and introducing them across the world. Governments played little role in all this, other than occasional inputs of capital to speed up implementation.

The process was not always tidy, and the world suffered more than one speculative boom and bust in the wake of some new technology. The conclusion, however, was Britain's leadership of the world, turning out one technology after another.

The Steam Railway

No mode of transport had so great an impact as the steam railway. As transport journalist Christian Wolmar has often argued, it is almost easier to list things thing that the invention of the railways *didn't* transform as those they did. Under the new railway network, ordinary people could for the first time travel across the country in a matter of hours, not days. Railways changed the nature of business, creating large new commercial organisations and setting the pattern for future industrial endeavours. They allowed milk to be delivered to cities from the countryside, and stopped the need for cows and other livestock to live within cities. They created mass tourism, allowing ordinary people to leave their home village or town for the first time.

---

11   This argument was initially put forward very convincingly by Mike Darwin on his Chronosphere blog at http://chronopause.com/index.php/2011/02/07/67/ (accessed on 3 March 2011)

Many were initially sceptical of the new technology. Nobody in human history had ever travelled so fast. The first riders worried it would be difficult to breathe at such speeds, or that the disturbance would hurt wildlife, causing horses to miscarry.[12] One writer in the *Quarterly Review* thought that steam trains travelling faster than stagecoaches was 'absurd and ridiculous', and argued for parliamentary regulation to limit their speed to eight or nine miles per hour.[13]

The first travellers soon discovered the new freedom that had been given to them outweighed any worries.

Steam travel opened such new realms of power – equivalent to six million horses or forty million men by 1870[14] – that it could be used on previously flippant indulgences. Even the workers could afford to travel for a day by the sea, or to visit relatives in the city. Fresh food could be delivered into the cities without spoiling.

The country became more closely bound together, allowing much faster communications. For the first time, it became necessary to set a common time zone for the whole country – no longer could a worker set his watch by the position of sun.

This rise of the railway was almost as rapid as it was revolutionary. The first line able to run steam engines, the Stockton and Darlington, opened in 1825 after engineer George Stephenson persuaded its backers of the potential of the technology. Carried upon the wave of a market boom, with investors desperate to get a piece of the new technology, railway lines soon crossed the country. In just twenty-two years, railways expanded from 100 miles in 1830 to 6,600 miles in 1852.[15]

---

12   Ridley, 2010 p. 283

13   Ibid., p. 284

14   Ibid., p. 231

15   Wolmar, *On the Wrong Line: How Ideology and Incompetence Wrecked Britain's Railways*, 2005, p. 5

This expansion was too rapid to be neat. With hindsight, the positioning of lines often seemed eccentric, or there was inefficient doubling up of lines. Trying to save costs, private builders would use frequent curves in the lines, sacrificing speed in the attempt to avoid difficult obstacles, or build their new stations in inconvenient locations away from the centre of cities.

Sometimes ambition got in the way of common sense, and many lines never made their money back. The Railway Mania was the first major financial bubble the country had seen since the South Sea Bubble. While the huge inputs of capital from ordinary people's savings allowed a rapid expansion of the network, many were to lose everything when the lines turned out to be unprofitable. Controversial figures such as the railway king George Hudson rapidly devised, raised funds for, and implemented new schemes, before buying up weaker rivals to build still bigger networks. Despite the bribery and corrupt accounting standards that were eventually to lead to his downfall and exile, it was ruthless, larger than life figures like Hudson who were often needed to push through the necessary schemes. His joint position as determined entrepreneur and lobbying politician gave him the influence needed to obtain the necessary planning permissions. At one point it was suggested he was trying to promise no fewer than sixteen different railway bills to his parliamentary colleagues.[16] He likely served as the inspiration for the dubious financier Augustus Melmotte in Trollope's novel *The Way We Live Now*.

The railway bubble collapsed in the late 1840s, like many other bubbles before and since. Yet the short-term losses to private investors were more than compensated by the long-term value the infrastructure provided to society as a whole.

---

16   Wolmar, *Fire and Steam: How the Railways Transformed Britain*, 2007

From the beginning, the railways were not entirely run on market forces, and government was to some extent involved. Each line required the passing of a new Act of Parliament to obtain the necessary planning permissions and the government was quick to pass a new tax in the Railway Passenger Duty. On failing in his attempt to nationalise key strategic lines in 1844 the then President of the Board of Trade Gladstone did succeed in making it compulsory for railway companies to offer Parliamentary Trains. Under this scheme, each operator had to offer at least one third-class train that stopped at all stations, its fares not exceeding one penny per mile.

Despite this, in contrast with what was to come later, the railways were a relatively free market in Britain, growing each year in passenger numbers and showing remarkable innovations in speed and comfort.

For much of the nineteenth century, Britain remained in the lead in railway expertise, exporting its engineers across the world.

Recognising the potential of the new technology, European powers frantically sought to create their own networks, if necessary with state support. The railways were more than a catalyst to economic growth – they were essential to a nation's military power. Before the creation of accurate aerial bombing, they were difficult to destroy but essential for logistical support. A. J. P. Taylor went so far as to argue in his 1969 *War by Timetable* that the immediate cause of the First World War was the railways timetables the opposing powers devised for mobilising their troops. The inflexible nature of the complex plans developed by the Russian and German general staffs meant that once mobilisation had begun the process could not easily be altered or stopped.

Railways could bind a country together, and allow armies to be dispatched in days rather than weeks, putting down rebellions such as the Indian Mutiny. It is no surprise that dictators such as the Russian Tsar were happy to pour money into the construction of titanic railways out east towards Siberia – understanding correctly that while it would never be an economic proposition, it would weave the new country together.

But then, it was the time for such grandiose projects. As often expressions of imperial audacity as commercial propositions, new railways crossed continents and overcame deserts, mountains, and rainforests. The British engineers who were often in charge, away from home years at a time, built new wonders of engineering – albeit at a heavy cost in human life. Accidents could be frequent, especially when trying to carve tunnels straight through the middle of a mountain, or worse, from illness. The rail historian George Tabor estimates, for example, that in its first two years of construction the new line between Fort Salisbury and the main Cape to Cairo line cost the lives of 400 of its white workforce (around 60 per cent), almost all 500 Indians, and one third of the African workers. Although the main killer was malaria, almost as dangerous was the local wildlife; losing a worker at night to the local lion population was a regular occurrence.[17]

It is easy to forget today, but another vast power that the railways helped to unify was America itself.

America's railways were soon to rival Britain's own.[18] Stimulated by furious competition, the new railroads quickly spread across the country, helping domesticate the old Wild West and putting an end to the old wagon routes such as the Oregon Trail. By 1869, the first transcontinental railroad had been built linking the east and west coasts. As in Britain, the business ethics and methods of competition were not always immaculate – this was the gilded era

---

17 Wolmar, *Blood, Iron and Gold: How the Railways Transformed the World*, 2009 p. 170

18 The relative merits seem to be a matter of understandable controversy between British and American rail historians.

in which the term 'robber baron' was popularised – but no matter the rail tycoon's ruthlessness, the networks they created succeeded in transforming the lives of their customers. Rail freight charges alone fell by 90 per cent between 1870 and 1900.[19]

Across the world, the railways changed economics, armies, lives and nations. For nearly a century they reigned supreme.

The Underground Railway

Perhaps nothing better represents the dynamism of Victorian Britain than the quest to solve the problems of London congestion.

As the centre of a rapidly growing world, London had been expanding rapidly, more than doubling in size to 2.5 million by 1850.[20] The influx of new people created traffic problems far beyond the capacity of horse-drawn omnibuses, but Parliament refused to allow the main railways to cut into the centre of the city.

The range of suggested solutions sounds, frankly, like something out of science fiction: trains powered by atmospheric pressure, a crystal railway enclosed in glass just below street level between St Paul's and Oxford Circus, or, alternatively, above ground in an arcade so spacious it could enclose houses and shops as well. Another suggestion was a cable railway, powered by a stationary engine pulling its carriages along a rope.

Or, just as crazy, a steam railway running under ground.

But nevertheless, that was exactly the option the 1854 Royal Commission went for. After incessant campaigning by social reformer Charles Pearson, they granted planning permission for a new railway line to be constructed underground between the northern London termini. To be fair, there were indeed significant early problems in the

---

19   Ridley, 2010 p. 23
20   Wolmar, *The Subterranean Railway*, 2004 p. 9

construction and after the opening of the network in 1863. Despite the ingenious use of vents out onto the streets, the engineers never fully solved the problem of running a steam engine through a cramped space. Many passengers struggled to breathe in the smoky, confined atmosphere.[21]

But nevertheless people kept coming. In only its first year of operation, nine million passengers used the new 'Metropolitan Railway'.[22] Just as incredibly, the network soon went through another two further huge innovations in technology. The initial cut-and-cover lines dug just below the street surface were joined by new lines dug deep under the ground, while in 1890 the steam problem was finally solved with the use of electricity to run the trains. Eventually the entire Tube system was electrified, a feat that we still haven't managed to replicate on the country's railway network as a whole.

Steam, Fuel and Electricity

The development of working steam engines at the turn of the nineteenth century opened many possibilities to entrepreneurial Victorian inventors. Simultaneous to the application of the new power on rails, other inventors were looking at possibilities on water.

The first prototype boat powered entirely by steam, the *Palmipède*, first sailed in 1776 in France, and progress continued rapidly until the *Charlotte Dundas*, perhaps the first practical steamboat, developed by William Symington in Glasgow in 1801. Within ten years, these paddle powered boats had entered commercial service on both sides of the Atlantic, although the limits of the technology and its insatiable need for fuel required them to stick mostly to inland waters.

The technology continued to develop. No one pushed it further than Isambard Kingdom Brunel. His 1838 ship the

21   Wolmar, *The Subterranean Railway,* 2004 p. 38
22   *The Victorian City* By H. J. Dyos, Michael Wolff p. 282

SS *Great Western* was the first steamship purpose-built for entirely steam powered crossings of the Atlantic. Indeed, the *Great Western* should have been the first ship to cross the Atlantic entirely on steam power, but was beaten by a rival, the SS *Sirius*. Unfortunately for the *Sirius*, this was only achieved with a three-day head start and the frantic burning of cabin furniture and a mast as fuel grew low. By contrast, the *Great Western* glided into port with 200 tons of coal to spare.

Brunel's second ship, the SS *Great Britain*, was if anything more revolutionary. Finished in 1845, the *Great Britain* was the first ocean-going vessel to combine steam power, an iron hull and the new screw propeller system, pioneered in 1839 by the SS *Archimedes*.

The combination of these three technologies revolutionised naval life, both commercially and militarily. It put an end to the 'Age of Sail' that had dominated European affairs since the Middle Ages. Eventually, the development of Sir Charles Parson's steam turbine engine, first prototyped in 1897 onboard the *Turbinia*, would lead to yet another generation of technology. However, this did have the effect of catalysing an arms race between Britain and Germany as the new Dreadnought class ships were launched.

Commercially, the dependability of steam power gave shipping a reliability and speed that it could never have enjoyed while still relying on the wind. Both the price of freight and the time it took for passengers to cross the oceans radically dropped.

Steam changed the look of our cities as well. Before the nineteenth century, buildings had been limited in height to around six floors. The combination of the new steam power, American inventor Elisha Otis's 1853 safety elevator and new building techniques brought about the age of the skyscraper. For the first time, cities could grow up as well as out.

But steam was only the first of three technologies that were to change fundamentally the way transport worked.

A problem with steam technology is that in burning the fuel away from the engine there results an inevitable loss of efficiency in the transfer of energy. By contrast, the internal combustion engine powers itself through the burning of the fuel right within the engine itself, pushing a piston and thus powering the motor. This allowed for smaller, more powerful engines.

Just as in the railways, developing an engine that was efficient and compact enough to power transport required a steady aggregation of different innovations in engineering and science. The modern form of the internal combustion owes most to the German Nikolaus Otto. His 1870s four-stroke engine provides the template still used today.

Finding the right fuel source proved to be no simpler. Early attempts envisioned the use of gunpowder, although this was quickly realised to be unpractical. Otto's engine was actually built to be powered by natural gas, but the pipelines required made this an impossibility for transport. It was the fortunate discovery of the by-product of kerosene refinement – petrol – that was to ensure the internal combustion engine's success.

Even more compact than petroleum was the last of the three new sources of power: electricity.

The first demonstration of electricity powering mechanical force was made by British scientist Michael Faraday as far back as 1821, and by the 1830s inventors across the world were building their own electric motors. None of them, however, would initially be able to make a commercial success of their invention due to the expense and poor capability of the day's battery technology.

Electricity only became practical as a power supply for transport after Thomas Edison had developed the idea of an electricity grid. While electricity allowed lighter, more nimble vehicles, it seemed most practical for vehicles that could be kept in constant contact with tracks.

These three technologies of steam, internal combustion and electricity were to define much of what was to come over the next hundred years. Gradually our transport methods have been undergoing a long-run transition, first from steam to internal combustion, and now in turn onto electricity. Ironically, steam's only use today is in the heart of some of our most advanced vehicles, nuclear powered submarines.

It was by no means initially obvious what application would suit which technology, and it was only a slow process of trial and error that made the right connections.

Take the example of cars. Throughout the nineteenth century, engineers experimented with different ways of replacing the horse with a carriage with a motor. As late as 1900, it was by no means clear whether steam, electric or petroleum cars would rule the future.

Britain was an early pioneer in the technology of steam cars, and saw vehicles running on the road as early as 1801. Over the next few decades the technology was refined until a combination of overreaching government regulation and careful lobbying by the competing railroads was to kill it off. The 1861 Locomotive Act enforced a four mph speed limit (or just two mph in towns), and required each vehicle to be preceded by a man carrying a red flag sixty yards in front of the vehicle.

Progress did continue overseas, and by the turn of the century there was a mix of steam, petroleum and electric vehicles available for purchase. Each had their advantages and disadvantages. Steam was quiet and could be fast – the Stanley Steamer set the world land speed record at 127.7 mph in 1906 – but needed a heavy engine, and required at least a few minutes to start while the engine heated up. Electric cars were quiet and convenient, but could only achieve limited speeds and were constrained in their range. Petroleum cars had more power, but needed difficult gear changes, and required hand cranking to start the motor. A bad backfire could break the operator's arm.

Where electricity did excel, however, was in its use for short distance transit.

By the middle of the nineteenth century, horse-driven trams were beginning to appear across the world. The clear advantage in rails came from the low friction of metal on metal, allowing the horses to pull heavier weights more easily, no matter the weather conditions. This made the trams much cheaper than horse-driven omnibuses, and more accessible to the working classes.

It was still expensive to provide the service, for each horse could only work so many hours a day and had to be carefully looked after. The conversion of the tramways to electricity by contrast, with each vehicle able to connect directly into the grid, allowed for vehicles that were light, efficient and cheap.

In retrospect it is amazing how quickly the age of the horse came to an end. In 1900 London still had 3,681 licensed horse-pulled buses and 1,473 trams. By 1915, there were only thirty-six horse-pulled buses and two trams.[23] The dominant form of land transport for millennia had been replaced in little more than a couple of decades.

The Twentieth Century

The end of the nineteenth century was not to see the end of the transport revolution. The twentieth century was to see yet more developments, as transport took to the skies. More than any other development, however, the story of transport in the twentieth century was dominated by the rise and rise of the automobile.

Despite its impact on ordinary life it is worth pointing out that many of the car's wider effects were not completely original. They built on earlier trends from one of the few

---

23 Bagwell & Lyth, 2002, p. 117

nineteenth-century transport inventions not to depend on steam, petrol or electric power: the humble bicycle.

The first forerunner to the modern bike was built by German Baron Karl von Drais in 1817. Using a simple wooden frame, its two wheels were powered directly by human motion. Initially conceived as a practical means to lessen the need for horses, their nickname of 'dandy horse' showed how quickly they became little more than a fad for wealthy fops. By 1860, the notion of pedals had significantly increased the technology's popularity and led to the golden (if often hazardous) age of the Penny Farthing bicycle.

By the start of the twentieth century, bicycles had reached their modern form with the creation of the 'safety bicycle'. Using a new rear chain drive, this allowed both effective speeds and wheels much closer to the ground.

Now safe and easy to ride, the popularity of bicycles rapidly spread, both for men and women. Bicycles helped to create a model for a new mechanised industry, the methods of assembly line production, and widespread advertising to drive demand. Aggressive lobbying by cyclist groups was to lead to the first government steps in improving the roads, which had been neglected since the emerging dominance of steam.

In the automobile market itself, the contest between steam, electric and petroleum power was eventually decided in favour of the fossil fuel. The invention of a small electric starter motor removed the need for hand cranking, while Henry Ford's perfection of assembly line processes for his 1908 Model T radically reduced prices.

As the century continued, petrol cars went from being a plaything for the rich to an essential that every family (and eventually adult) expected to own. In 1913 in the United States there was one car for every hundred people. By 1922, after Ford had halved their cost, one in ten could expect to own their own automobile. By 1950, there were 50 million cars in America, or one for every three people.[24]

Just as the railways a century before, the rise of the car altered the way we lived. It changed the daily habits of families, giving them more freedom to roam, and opening the possibility of new supermarkets and retail centres. Their architectural impact was immense, completely reshaping the look and feel of cities. As architectural critic Reyner Banham quipped, he learned to drive so that he could read Los Angeles in the original.[25]

But their impact was less positive on the methods of transport they replaced. Just as the original railways had made the old turnpike system unviable, the new cars in turn would cause immense difficulties for the railways. Some transport methods like the trams disappeared almost entirely.

In response to this new competition the railways accelerated their already ongoing consolidation. In Britain they merged to such an extent that by the 1920s there were only the so-called 'Big Four' railway companies left: Great Western; London, Midland and Scotland; Southern; and London and North Eastern.

The coming of the First World War was to be a catalyst for much change, in the railways as everything else. The concentration of the railways made it easier for the government to take over the operation of the industry, on the grounds that they were a strategically necessary asset. This imposed enormous strain on the infrastructure that the government never fully compensated the railway companies for. Neither was the industry helped outside war by restrictive regulation of their freight business, which limited their rate of return and forced them to carry unprofitable cargo. Such a system might have made sense in the days when

---

24   O'Toole, 2009, p. 15
25   Banham, Reyner, *Los Angeles The Architecture Of Four Ecologies.* Harper and Row 1971

rail held an effective monopoly, but they now faced increasing competition from road haulage. At the same time, they faced falling demand from new consumer industries that no longer required such bulk transport.

The desperate search for an edge in combat encouraged massive technological innovation in transport. By the end of the war, the new tanks had begun to make a difference against the machine gun and trench warfare. The development of submarines – a concept that had been toyed with since Greek times – was to show the chaos that disruption of normal transport routes could bring.

A more optimistic development was another vehicle that was to make gigantic leaps forward during the war: the aeroplane.

Throughout the nineteenth century, inventors had explored different technologies both for gliders and the engines that could power them into flight. Experiments in the world's first wind tunnel by British engineer Francis Herbert Wenham in the 1870s proved that heavier than air flight was possible, but it took until 1903 before the constant experiments of the American Wright brothers proved a success. The Wright brothers' jealous protection of their patents held back progress in their own county, and the centre of innovation instead shifted to Europe. Progress continued rapidly, especially under the extreme pressures brought about by war.

After the war, several new commercial airlines were formed, but it soon became clear that costs were far too high in the fledgling technology for the business to be economical. By 1921 all the British airlines had been forced out of business, while foreign competitors had their profits guaranteed by their respective governments. Unwilling for the UK to fall behind, the government began looking into its own subsidy regime. By 1924, it had decided that the existing four airlines should be merged into a single firm, the new Imperial Airways.

Thus was set in place the pattern that was to bedevil international aviation over the next century. As each country supported its own flag carrier, it was impossible for any airline to go bankrupt. Competition could only drive prices down, pushing them far below what the airlines needed to make a profit. As late as 2003, *The Economist* magazine could complain that airlines had never succeeded in their sixty years in earning a return on their capital.[26]

Despite sheer gains in speed, passenger demand for aviation remained low for the first few decades, held back as much by comfort and perceived safety as cost. For those who preferred a more stable ride, there was also the German-pioneered Zeppelin, one of the reasons for the distinctive shape of the Empire State Building: its owners argued for it to be used as a landing terminal for the craft.[27]

While technological progress continued, it soon became clear that there were fundamental limits to what could achieved through a propeller and piston-based engine.

Determined to be a pilot ever since he was a child, the inventor of the jet engine Frank Whittle was as brilliant and daring in his engineering as he was in the air. Throughout the 1930s he doggedly pushed his idea of a jet-based turbine engine despite almost unanimous official scepticism. Only after he had raised enough venture capital to develop a prototype engine in 1937 did the Air Ministry take an interest in funding.

The first British jet plane, the *Gloster Meteor*, finally flew in 1943, although by this time a German, Hans von Ohain, had independently developed a jet engine of his own. Later

---

26   'Open Skies and Flights of Fancy', 2 October 2003, available at http://www.economist.com/node/2099875

27   'Not Just a Perch for King Kong', 23 September 2010, New York Times, accessed 22 April 2011, available at http://www.nytimes.com/2010/09/26/realestate/26scapes.html

in life, when both had moved to America, the two inventors of the jet were to become good friends.

The jet plane was just the last in a long series of innovations. By the beginning of the Second World War the world's transport systems had entered a golden age with a wide variety of modes: automobiles and steam trains for land; buses, trams and a newly electrified Underground for the cities; ocean liners and submarines at sea; aeroplanes and Zeppelins for the sky.

Comet and Concorde

For a brief moment, in the ten years that followed the Second World War, Britain continued her lead in aviation innovation.[28]

The memories of the Spitfire's triumph in the Battle of Britain still vivid, a vast array of manufacturers sought to ensure Britain's triumph in the new Jet Age, and to scale the seemingly insurmountable sound barrier. Vast crowds turned out year after year for the Farnborough Air Show to see the latest wares, even after the horrific accident in 1952, when twenty-seven people were killed by the wreckage of an imploding de Havilland 110 fighter falling into the crowd.

Inevitably, the most cutting edge technology was developed for military purposes. Not only had the war shown the necessity of air superiority, but, in the years before the deployment of ICBMs, bombers were an integral part of an effective nuclear deterrent.

But Britain was a poor country in the wake of the conflict. Struggling with the debts built up, it could no longer afford continued massive expenditure on the air force. Looking to make savings, the government suspended development on military aircraft. As, it declared, there was no conceivable

---

28 James Hamilton-Paterson provides a very readable account of the times in his 2010 book *Empire of the Clouds*.

possibility of war in the next ten years, the RAF and Navy could do without new fighters until at least 1957.[29]

Whatever the military reasons, the pause was to prove fatal for Britain's technological lead. Advanced projects such as the 1,000 mph turbojet M.52 were quietly cancelled.

In civil aviation, Britain had also enjoyed a brief ascendancy. The de Havilland Comet was the world's first jet airliner, entering commercial service as early as 1952 and cutting flight times in half.

But then disaster struck.

Two Comets failed to leave the runway – accidents initially blamed on pilot error, but later discovered to be the result of a flaw in the design of the wing profile. Worse, over the next two years a further two aircraft were to experience complete structural failure mid air, taking the lives of their passengers and crew.

The aircraft was grounded while the faults were investigated, but by 1958, when the problems with the pressurisation of the cabin had been resolved, Britain had lost its technological edge. The same year planes from foreign competitors such as the Boeing 707 or the Douglas DC-8 were launched, designs with which the older plane could never compete.

It is difficult to know who to blame for the downfall of the British aviation industry. The technological flaws were inexcusable, but then there are always problems with new technology. In many ways the industry struggled to make the transition away from wartime to the more modest demands of peace.

The coming of the jet plane completely transformed the nature of tourism, radically increasing capacity. By shuttling back and forth, even the relatively small 707 could carry as many passengers as the *Queen Mary* ocean liner.[30]

---

29   Hamilton-Paterson, 2010 p. 55

30   Sampson, 1984, p. 111

By 1957, there were already more passengers crossing the Atlantic by air than sea, and traffic then doubled every five years.[31]

While there only had ever been a relatively small number of the great ships, there were soon hundreds of planes crossing the sky. The only way to fill up all the capacity was with a radical expansion of travel, far beyond what the airlines had initially predicted. The age of mass foreign tourism was born.

Looking to surpass the 707, the British and French governments joined forces in the pursuit of a new supersonic jet liner: the Concorde.

Supersonic jets were widely assumed to be the future of commercial aviation, in just the same way that they'd become the norm in the military arena. Learning of the advanced state of the European plans, even the American government panicked. President John Kennedy went so far as to promise to subsidise up to 75 per cent of the development costs of Boeing and Lockheed's own supersonic projects.

But creating a supersonic plane with the needed scale, efficiency and range proved a more difficult proposition than had initially been expected. The smaller streamlined body and lower fuel efficiency of the jet meant that the plane required up to five times as much fuel per passenger as subsonic planes. Fundamentally different engineering is needed for below and above the sound barrier, and the plane inevitably had to be a compromise between the two. While faster, the planes could still only make the trip back and across the Atlantic once a day, meaning there was little financial advantage to the operators. Worse, the backlash from its noise pollution resulted in it being banned from operating at supersonic speeds anywhere other than above the ocean. This fatally restricted the routes that the service had a speed advantage on, and was to be the undoing of its

---

31   Sampson, 1984, p. 110

commercial ambitions. The project only ever later achieved limited profitability when it was positioned as an extremely premium service, with ticket prices to match.

Instead, the future was to belong to Boeing's 747, introduced in 1969. A giant of an aeroplane, able to carry over 500 passengers, it was initially intended by its developer only as a temporary solution. Boeing assumed that the future for passenger service belonged to supersonic jets, but believed that the 747s, with their distinctive hump-like upper deck, could be easily convertible into cargo planes where speed would be much less important.

They were wrong. Boeing's own supersonic project, the 2707, was cancelled, while the latest model of the 747, the 747-8, is due for delivery to its first customers in mid 2011. The temporary solution has survived forty years.

But then the age of transport innovation itself was coming to an end. The jet liner was to be the last significant transport innovation to carry passengers. Trains continued their slow conversion from steam to diesel to electricity, and a few countries experimented with new high speed networks to better compete with flights. Cars continued to grow more reliable and safer, although increasing congestion limited the speed gains that could be achieved.

Only in space would we see the doing of things that hadn't been possible before – and that, in harmony with the age, would be dominated by the state.

The Rise and Fall of Planning

While the story of the nineteenth century was largely private-sector led, the twentieth century was to see the rise of government. Planning would dominate the scene.

During the Second World War, the government again took much of Britain's transport industry under direct control, but, this time, it did not return it back to the market after the war had ended. The railways were merged into a new British Railways, and the airlines reorganised into the twin British Overseas Airlines Company and British Europeans Airlines. Even road haulage was nationalised under the all powerful British Transport Commission.

In 1953, the Conservative government made some moderate reforms to this system, returning haulage back into private control and reorganising control of the railways. For the most part, however, they accepted the new settlement of government control in transport.

One of the advantages of this was that the government began a programme of massive investment in the roads, hoping to create a national network of motorways to rival the autobahns in Germany or freeways in America. The first road, the M6 Preston Bypass, opened in 1958, and the government then continued to expand the network throughout the next thirty years. Despite this encouraging development, it should be noted that in the 1930s the government actively prevented private investors from building their own motorways.

The continuing and growing success of the roads had its problems. The government tried to build enough capacity to stay ahead of congestion in a policy that became known as predict-and-provide, but never acted fast enough to prevent traffic jams in the city centres.

As the success of cars grew, the railways struggled as passenger numbers plummeted and freight fled to the unregulated roads. In 1955, the government attempted to stem the ongoing losses with an ambitious Modernisation Plan to bring back passengers to the railways. It called for a new generation of stations and trains, and a conversion to diesel and electric power to restore ongoing profitability.

The plan failed. Passenger revenue and freight revenue continued to drop, and it became increasingly obvious that, aside from spending more money, there were no strategic ideas on how to improve service quality or attract customers back.

Accepting the inevitable, government policy began to see the railways as in a period of managed decline. Burdened with the costs of a vast network built for Victorian levels of demand, the railway were simply uneconomical – but even moderate attempts to prune them back such as the 1960s Beeching cuts proved vastly controversial. As a government-owned institution, raising fares was often politically difficult, if not impossible.

Meanwhile, the air industry enjoyed steady growth, although Britain never was to regain its post-war lead. The initial primary airport of Croydon was recognised as unsuitable for future development, constrained by a shortage of land, and development consequently moved to a new site at Heathrow in 1946. Meanwhile Britain's two state airlines were merged in 1974 into the new British Airways, while other independent airlines such as British Caledonian managed to find a niche for themselves – this despite government regulation limiting its ability to compete in markets where British Airways already operated.

It was the United States who were to start the privatisation movement which was to so change transport. Over the 1970s the Nixon, Ford and Carter administrations between them would introduce acts liberalising trucking, rail and aviation.

The liberalisation of aviation in 1978 was the first and perhaps most dramatic change. Many of the old American firms such as Pan Am and TWA did not survive the transition to the new era, but the result was a far more competitive sector. Traffic increased by over 150 per cent, while over 80 per cent of passengers enjoyed lower fares.[32] New business models were explored. Rather than try to offer every route direct, airlines realised they could serve a far broader market by first flying you from local airports into a

---

32   'Open Skies and Flights of Fancy', 2 October 2003, available at
       http://www.economist.com/node/2099875

regional hub instead. A new range of low cost carriers such as Southwest Airlines offered discount prices.

Results in the railways were almost as dramatic. For many decades, the railways had struggled, many companies going bankrupt. It was simply not possible to run a profit while restrained by government controls on prices and services, and in particular by the loss making passenger trains they were forced to run. The US 1980s Staggers Act did away with all this, and in the process was to create arguably the world's leading rail freight market. Productivity levels, which had stood still for decades, have risen by 172 per cent since, while rates halved.[33] In sharp contrast, the US continued to lag behind the rest of the world when it came to shipping, held back by the protectionism of the 1920s Jones Act, which mandated that domestic cargo had to be carried and built by US facilities.[34] In 1948, over a third of commercial ships were American. Today it is less than 2 per cent.[35]

In Britain, transport was similarly one of the sectors to be most radically affected by the privatisation agenda of Margaret Thatcher's Conservative administration in the 1980s. The government began by privatising freight, Associated British Ports and Jaguar, hoping to achieve the same success they had enjoyed with the privatisation of British Telecom.

The first major sector to be privatised was the buses. In the wake of the 1985 Transport Act, Transport Secretary Nicholas Ridley implemented a breakup of the National Bus Company into over seventy separate local bus companies. Ultimately, this level of diversity would soon prove unsustainable, and most of these smaller units quickly consolidated into bigger organisations.

---

33   http://www.economist.com/node/16636101
34   http://www.ft.com/cms/s/0/024650d6-3f92-11e0-
      a1ba-00144feabdc0.html#axzz1G63J9QYT
35   http://www.nytimes.com/2007/01/02/opinion/02perry.html

The air industry was next to be liberalised. The British Airports Authority was privatised whole in 1986 as BAA Plc, with the expectation that this would increase its ability to raise private capital for greater investment. Shortly after, in 1987, British Airways followed. In the run up to privatisation Sir John King had led a remarkably successful programme to cut costs and return the company to profitability, and by the early 1990s the company even enjoyed a brief period of success as 'the world's favourite airline'.

The privatisation programme was largely seen as a success, generating new competition. Throughout the 1970s, aviation entrepreneur Freddie Laker had sought to create a new SkyTrain service, offering flights across the Atlantic at a third of the going rate. After six years of constant negotiation on both sides of the Atlantic, SkyTrain was finally granted a licence and launched to huge initial success. Passengers queued overnight to obtain tickets, while *Time* magazine went so far as to put Laker's face on its front cover. Despite this early success, in 1982 Laker Airways went spectacularly bust, unable to keep up with its own over ambitious plans for expansion or a controversial 1981 agreement between BA and Pan Am for drastic fare cuts to match Laker's rates. Partly a result of this, in 1981–2 BA lost as much as £144 million,[36] but then, directly backed by government loans, it could afford to make such losses.

Nevertheless, Laker's lead was soon followed by other companies such as Virgin Atlantic and the low cost carriers Easyjet and Ryanair. Mindful of his experience fighting the establishment, Sir Freddie Laker memorably instructed Richard Branson of Virgin, 'When BA come after you, which they inevitably will, shout long, shout hard and then sue the bastards!'[37] In return, Branson was later to name one of Virgin's Boeing 747s *The Spirit of Sir Freddie*.

---

36   Sampson, 1984 p. 159
37   http://www.time.com/time/europe/hero2006/laker.html

Privatisation in the railways was to suffer from longer lasting problems. By the 1980s British Rail had improved on many of its earlier faults. New generations of High Speed Trains were providing efficient connections between cities at a much lower cost than the French and Japanese solutions of dedicated high speed rail lines. Passenger numbers were increasing, while the relatively low level of subsidy made British Rail one of the most efficient railways in the world.[38]

Having to start from a single monolithic national company, the government attempted to create new markets by dividing up British Rail into its core functions; new companies were established for operating trains, holding the stock and maintaining the infrastructure. Yet, despite the theoretical benefits such competition should bring, they were unable to prevent massive increases in costs and subsequent subsidy.

Meanwhile, the continued race to meet demand for new roads struggled. Academics began to insist that no increase in capacity could ever meet seemingly inexorable demand. At the same time, environmental concerns over the cost to the natural landscape and global environment became more pressing, especially in the wake of a series of highly controversial protests at the sites of new roads.

Despite the changes it wrought, the privatisation wave of the late twentieth century provided at best a check to, rather than a complete reversal of, the nationalisation experiment. Through its tight control of regulation, land planning and franchising processes, the government remains in firm control of the progress of transport. Indeed, many systems seem now so tied up with government that it is far from clear how Britain could return to a private system even if wanted to.

---

38   Wolmar, *On the Wrong Line: How Ideology and Incompetence Wrecked Britain's Railways*, 2005, p. 44

Lessons from History

If one lesson stands out clearly from the past, it is the sheer unpredictability of progress. Technical advances arrive abruptly rather than in a steady linear trend. Horses disappeared in a decade or two. The railways expanded in barely much longer. While technological progress is a product of steady evolution and the accumulation of ideas, the point at which a technology becomes practical can arrive with astonishing speed and leave companies and governments completely unprepared.

Not only do we find it almost impossible to predict which technology will prove essential and which will be an expensive dead end, but we also find it impossible to conceive beforehand what uses we'll make of technology before it is developed. Cars are not just horseless wagons. The Underground didn't only relieve congestion, it changed the very nature of the city itself. When given the opportunity, it turned out that ordinary people didn't want to spend their lives trapped in their home village or county, but wanted to travel further and faster. The Victorians discovered the 'day by the seaside', the generation of the 1960s and 1970s the package holiday.

It is tempting to suggest that nearly all transport innovation has come from the private sector. While government subsidy and, in particular, military funding has provided heavy support for early technologies, the real paradigm shifts have come from the private world. It is difficult for a central bureaucracy to justify the risk and expense of a tentative new project when the current system is seen to be working well. Frank Whittle had to struggle hard to get the establishment to pay attention to his invention of the jet engine, while the railways barely progressed under government control. The roads have always been in government hands, and never seemed to be on the verge of trying anything fundamentally new.

Indeed, ever since the government took control of transport, the great paradigm changes seem to have disappeared altogether. Is it coincidence that the rise of planning and the end of the transport revolution coincided?

We should not push this point too far. We understand so little about what caused the upsurge in entrepreneurialism in Victorian England in the first place that it is difficult to say what could have prevented its dynamism continuing in any particular sector. None of us can know what would have happened in an alternate history where government did not take complete control.

As recent commentators have argued, technological progress seems to have slowed down across the entire economy after the war, at least away from the narrow areas of computing and communications.[39] Cars have remained, more or less, out of government hands, and yet the nature of the vehicle has not radically changed in the last fifty years.

It may be that we were simply fortunate in the beginning, taking advantage of the relatively straightforward application of the new powers of steam, chemicals and electricity. It was once thought that the next stage would be nuclear powered trains and cars, but health and security risks made that impractical. We have now reached the limits of our current technologies, and are struggling against the limits of physics for ever more marginal improvements. The physical nature of resistance means that it takes ever more power to gain greater speed, but we have discovered no new sources of power to push us past this limit. We would have happily electrified our automobile fleet a long time ago if only we could overcome the limitations of our battery technology.

But then, it is as often necessity that produces great advances in technology as progress in science. While we may not be in a position to build a flying car, there is a vast range of possibilities that remain both within the reach of today's science and are completely untried. The example of

---

39   For a good summary of the argument, see Cowen, Tyler. *The Great Stagnation*. Penguin 2011

the Roman hot-air balloon that never was, or the railways that were never developed, reminds us that it is not always technology that holds the progress of a society back.

It is at least possible that one reason the rate of progress in our transport industries is closer to that in health and education than computing is that the former remains centrally controlled, while the latter enjoys the freedom and entrepreneurialism of the market. Our transport systems have been fossilised in rigid government plans, their future expansion decided on the predicted demand thirty years in the future. The natural correlative of Stalinist-style planning is Stalinist-style lack of innovation.

It would be unfair to claim that the nationalisation movement had no successes. Despite its many faults, Heathrow is one of the busiest airports in the world. Expansions of the Underground such as the Jubilee Line Extension proved a great success, and many other world cities have looked enviously at London's integrated system of public transport and congestion charging. A brand new motorway network was envisioned, planned and constructed to great public success.

Nevertheless, even planning's greatest adherents have to admit that much of the last fifty years seems to have been wasted. The cumulative damage from underinvestment has been significant. Britain's roads remain congested, while huge sums of money are being poured into the railways to get them into a workable state. It is tempting for today's transport activists to be nostalgic about the recent past, but the truth is that nationalised transport services did not achieve the co-ordinated, strategic results they promised.

As we will soon see, the twentieth-century version of transport is rapidly becoming out of date. It is simply unable to cope with the coming challenges of congestion and climate change. Our only hope is to rediscover the entrepreneurial drive of the Victorians – but that will be impossible while transport remains dominated by the Planners.

THE PROBLEM WITH PLANNING

Britain Lay in Ruins

The country's future had never looked so perilous. Across seas, thousands of soldiers were daily giving their lives. Buildings lay scattered in the rubble they had been reduced to by Nazi bombs. Hungry mothers and children queued, ration book in hand, to receive their weekly shop.

And yet, despite the chaos and war that persisted outside, within the warm confines of the Civil Service bureaucrats had begun the task of looking at what came after. New nationalised industries, a National Health Service – and the country's first motorway network.

First conceived during the war, and eventually published in 1946 by the Ministry of War Transport, the map 'Showing Future Pattern of Principal National Routes' was little more than a rough sketch, and yet was to prove an eerily accurate prototype of the network that was to come.

Despite everything that was to change over the next fifty years – the loss of an Empire, changes in government, oil crises, new environmental protests – this map proved a good guide. By the time motorway building had largely been abandoned by the early 1990s, the vision was virtually complete.

Unlike the chaotic manner in which Britain's railway network had scattered its way over the country, here was an example of good Continental-style long-term strategic thinking. The needs of the country had been estimated, and facilities put in place to provide for them.

If only all our economy was this logical – what more proof was needed that planning was the way forward?

The Planning Revolution

By the end of World War II, a revolution in the way we thought about politics had brought about the era of Big Government. The State was to take direct responsibility for its population's health, education and jobs, nationalising the leading industries in the country and ensuring prosperity for all.

Transport was no different. In October 1940 the Transport Minister was Sir John Reith. Having been the first Director General of the BBC, famously declaring its mission to 'education, inform, entertain', Reith was already familiar with the benefits that could supposedly be achieved by nationalised industries. He asked his civil servants to write a report on the 'problem of transport' in Great Britain, and proposing the establishment of a National Transport Corporation as its solution. Throughout the war, work on this theme continued, eventually leading to the Transport Act in 1947.

The man who led the task was a respected former civil servant, William Coates. Coates was a hard working man, obtaining degrees in both Economics and Law from the London School of Economics while at the same time making his way up through the ranks of the Civil Service. In the mid 1920s he moved across to the private sector, and became a pivotal figure as a director in the newly formed Imperial Chemistry Industries (ICI). His fellow directors respected his intellect, although he could be apparently prone to writing 'donnish papers.'[40]

Hard working and clever, Coates was in no doubt about the importance of his task. As his introduction to the 1942 report stated: 'Every trade, business and industry in the country is dependent on transport; every man, woman and child needs its services. It is the handmaiden of both industry and leisure.'[41] It was imperative to ensure that

---

40   Coates, Sir William Henry, *Oxford Dictionary of National Biography*, accessed April 2011

41   Coates, July 1942, p. 2

the 'transport industry should be maintained by efficient management and wise administration at the highest possible standard of efficiency'.[42]

This problem, he believed, could be achieved with a thoroughly non partisan report, a 'reasoned and dispassionate survey, from a transport and business point of view, and not from any political angle'.[43]

Within the very next sentence of his report, Coates spells out his supposed pragmatic solution, 'the adoption of a comprehensive scheme for the unification, under a public service corporation, of all the means of internal transport'.[44] This would allow the 'the elimination of uneconomic or even economic competition'.[45] After all, 'Co-ordination is a blessed word.'[46]

Coates and other civil servants struggled for months with the various difficult technical questions thrown up by the unification. They had to be careful to calculate the most efficient solution and division of functions, a task they were sure could never be achieved by the market. As Coates said,

> The functions required of transport are too variable, not only with the conditions in different areas, but also with the almost infinite variety of goods to be carried and the conditions of the time, even down to the conditions of an individual trader. It follows that the end envisaged cannot be attained by free competition.[47]

He and his fellow report writer Sir Alfred Robinson were under no illusions as to what this would require. In an

---

42   Coates, July 1942, p. 2
43   Ibid., p. 2
44   Ibid., p. 2
45   Ibid., p. 18
46   Ibid., p. 18
47   Ibid., p. 23

earlier memo to Reith, Robinson agreed that while it was probably best to 'to leave untouched the "private" car' they should 'abolish, the present right of the trader (whether he be the Cement Marketing Board or the village grocer) to use his own goods vehicle.'[48] Instead, 'the Corporation would in its unfettered discretion decide on means of transport and route'.[49]

In the end, Coates and Robinson were to get most of what they wanted. Encouraged by its experience during war, the government took over the railways, airports, airlines, buses, underground, freight and ports. Industries that had initially been created under the initiative of private entrepreneurs were now to be placed under the control of a central bureaucracy.

Of course, the theory that central planning was more efficient than market practice was not a new one. Government and the private sector have always traded back and forth their relative influence on transport. For centuries, roads had been the responsibility of central government, although occasionally control was passed over to turnpike operators.

The extent of planning in the rail industry had varied widely in the nineteenth century. While international leaders Britain and the US had largely left the railways to private entrepreneurs, countries such as Belgium ran a totally state controlled system. Still others, such as France and Germany, had tried a hybrid solution, using the state to deliver the most important routes, while letting the private sector fill out the rest of the gaps.

In contrast, during the twentieth century government took the definite lead across the world. On the roads, it was government that was responsible for the creation of new motorway and freeway networks. The emerging aviation

---

48   Letter from A. T. V. Robinson to the Minister for Transport (Sir John Reith), 1940

49   Ibid.

industry was soon entangled in international negotiations, as most countries set up their own nationalised flag carriers. The private railways of the nineteenth century passed into government hands, as even the US nationalised its struggling railroads in the 1970s into the new entity of Amtrak.

The twentieth-century experiment with planning has not been a success. It turns out that government monopolies are just as inefficient, if not more so, than private ones. They are slow to change, unresponsive to passengers and often expensive. The efficiencies that Coates and his colleagues foresaw have not come to pass. Government planners have proved incapable of keeping up with the wider changes in our society.

It is perhaps understandable that at the height of wartime planning well meaning government bureaucrats put so much faith in their own ability to control a whole industry. While the draconian restrictions on individuals' freedom to move their own goods now horrify, such moves may not have seemed so drastic in a time of rationing and security restrictions.

But while the rest of the world moved on and rediscovered the virtues of free markets, transport planners still seem stuck in that same mindset of the 1940s. As we will see, they still argue that transport is just too important and too complex to be left to the market alone. They still believe in total nationalisation as a non partisan technocratic solution, and exult the virtues of Coates's 'blessed' co-ordination over the wastefulness of competition.

Today, the ultimate mission of transport planners is to move us away from polluting, individualistic cars to green, public transport. 'I will have failed... if in five years there are not many more people using public transport and far fewer journeys by car,' announced John Prescott in June 1997 on the launch of his new more 'integrated' transport policy. (He did). 'It is a tall order but I want you to hold me to it.'

New Labour's new policy of a more co-ordinated transport policy was met with enthusiasm by the planner community. 'It was an incredibly exciting period – it was a revolution,' recalled Professor David Begg ten years later, who earlier had chaired the Commission For Integrated Transport. 'There was that feeling', agrees Professor Phil Goodwin, once head of transport studies at Oxford University, 'I had it personally and a lot of people associated with the re-thinking of transport policy felt the same thing... a feeling that yes, this was the first time maybe that professionals and politicians were seeing eye to eye.'[50]

While Planners soon became disillusioned with New Labour, in particular after the 2000 Fuel Duty protests forced backing off from earlier plans, they should not be too disheartened. While the rest of our economies have rediscovered the benefits of free competition and private ownership, transport networks remain largely under government control. After all, Planners argue, transport is just too complicated to be under the control of anything but the wisest of government bureaucrats.

The Planning of Tokyo

Tokyo is, by popular acclaim, one of the world's three leading cities, the motor at the heart of the Asian economy.[51] The city itself contains over 8 million people, but what really gives it its strength is the integration of a further 30 million into the world's largest metropolitan area. These people in turn support the world's largest metropolitan economy, valued at a GDP of US $1.479 trillion in 2008.[52] That's nearly the same size as the entire economy of Britain.

---

50   http://news.bbc.co.uk/1/hi/magazine/8465383.stm

51   Foreign Policy Global Cities Index 2010 - http://www.foreignpolicy. com/articles/2010/08/11/the_global_cities_index_2010 - retrieved 3 March 2010

52   'Global city GDP rankings 2008-2025'. Pricewaterhouse Coopers https://www.ukmediacentre.pwc.com/imagelibrary/downloadMe-dia.ashx?MediaDetailsID=1562 – retrieved 3 March 2010

To make such a powerful economy work, all those 38 million people need to be able to move conveniently from home to work to friends and back again. To make an effective transport system that can support such movements is surely a logistical challenge beyond human understanding.

Which is perhaps why in 2009 a group of Japanese researchers from Hokkaido University experimented with the services of a somewhat different type of transport planner.

A world-leading transport planning expert, exhibiting a glittering career of academic prizes and a CV to match?

No.

Perhaps a new advanced computer model, run by the latest Japanese supercomputers, juggling thousands of specified variables in a careful attempt to simulate the future?

Not at all.

What the Japanese researchers actually used was a well chosen variety of slime mould – a species of amoeba known as *Physarum polycephalum*.[53]

The researchers painstakingly created a map of the Toyko metropolitan area on a wet surface, using oat flakes for major cities and spots of bright light to represent mountain ranges or other geological features that would need to be avoided.

The mould was then left to its own devices, spreading out to reach food and doing its best to avoid the bright light. Using a process of trial and error, it reinforced routes that seemed to work well and abandoned those it found that it didn't need. The researchers wanted to see what sort of network the mould could evolve, left to itself.

What the researchers soon discovered was that the end result was a network that not only nearly matched the real Tokyo train system, but was in many ways more efficient.

---

53 Rules for Biologically Inspired Adaptive Network Design, Tero, et al., Science 22 January 2010: 439-442.DOI:10.1126/science.1177894

No central planner. No complex models built on thousand of variables.

Perhaps planning wasn't so essential after all?

Intelligent Design and Markets

The lesson of the above example is not that we should pass control of the Tube network from the planners at Transport for London to the mould that lurks in its dark tunnels.

The key observation is that what looks like planning doesn't always actually have to be planned. Ever since Darwin, we've known this to be true in the animal kingdom. Something as complicated as the human eye may seem to be a miracle. How did we end up with the ultimate in 3D, HD video camera technology without a designer? The answer is a long process of natural selection and evolution. Indeed, computer scientists Dan Nilsson and Susanne Pelger have managed to simulate the evolution of a complex eye from simple light-sensitive skin in no more than a few hundred thousand generations.[54] Given enough time or enough scale, complex systems can evolve from the seeming random interplay of disparate individuals.

What is true in biology is true in the human world as well. Societies and economies evolve as individuals look for the best way to save time, earn more money, or impress their peers. Economists from Adam Smith to Freidrich Hayek have argued for the power of collections of individuals, making their own free choices, to achieve ends that work out for the greater good.

This is just as true in transport as it is anywhere else. Nobody planned the invention of the railway or the internal combustion engine. Over time entrepreneurs experimented with different ways to move people around. Some of these

---

54   Referenced in *How the Mind Works*, Steven Pinker, Penguin, 1997,
      p. 164

proved huge successes, and so became part of everyday life, while others disappeared in failure.

Planning is 'intelligent design' applied to markets. Intuitively tempting, but ultimately not the way progress happens.

Five Myths about Planning

The reputation of free markets has taken a severe denting in the years since the economic crisis. Transport planners join many other critics who argue that free markets left to themselves ignore our concerns over equality, pollution, safety and monopoly. Markets don't always work in practice as well as theory suggests.

One of the worst complaints against free market theory has been *homo economicus*, the supposedly perfectly rational, but selfishly amoral character, who lurks at the centre of this view of economics.

Real people we know aren't like that. They make mistakes and rarely think too far ahead about the consequences of their decisions. They care about other people, looking after their friends and family, and sending the occasional donation to charity. They're as worried about their status and standing in society as the exact number on their pay cheque.

The problem with planning is that these real people are just as far from *homo planicus* as they are *homo economicus*.

Planners rely on just as unrealistic picture of the way society works as any neoliberal economist. The idea of the wise government bureaucrat pointing us in the right direction may be as old as Plato's philosopher kings, but no more accurate now than it was in the classical world. The real government isn't dominated by all-knowing, selfless public servants in the pursuit of the public good, just as free markets don't always adjust instantly or perfectly to some social equilibrium.

Planners are just as prone to arrogance as the rest of us, to looking after special interests and overestimating their own abilities. They have no perfect source of knowledge, pointing them to the right thing to do. They have to guess.

In the real world, we always have to balance off the relative advantages and flaws of markets and plans. The lessons we appear to have learned from our experiments over the last hundred years are that we do not need perfect competition to gain some benefits from competition, nor perfect incentives for prices to be useful. Markets have many flaws, but they seem to do a far better job than plans in being responsive to customers, restraining costs and innovating with new ideas.

Once we move past the cartoon world of flawed markets and a perfect planning system, many of the reasons for planning's supremacy evaporate.

Here are five myths that no longer seem as convincing:

Myth One: Transport is too important to be left to the market

Transport is the handmaiden of both industry and leisure... Because it is a universal need, transport is an industry in which the public industry is predominant.
Dr W. H. Coates, 'Report on The Transport Problem in Great Britain'[55]

Despite transport's importance to the process of industrialisation, it is more than just another sector of the economy. Rather it is a piece of national infrastructure, of equal importance to schools, hospitals, the police force and other vital institutions without which modern society cannot function... transport is a public service which cannot be allowed to malfunction through lack of funds...
Philip Bagwell and Peter Lyth, *Transport in Britain*[56]

---

55   Coates, July 1942
56   Bagwell & Lyth, 2002 pp. XII–XIII

Every week or so, most of us visit our local supermarket. Laid out there in front of us for our selection are the harvests of dozens of nations. Millions of workers have toiled fields to grow and harvest crops, which are then distributed by ships, lorries and bored part-time workers onto the shelf in front of you. There can be few items more essential to the continuing of our existence than a secure, ample food supply – and yet, with the exception of a few misconceived attempts to tinker with the price, we largely leave the market alone.

This, of course, is a miracle of everyday life, and hardly the sole province of food. One famous academic paper showed that when we have taken the full distribution chain into account, as basic an item as a pencil can be the end result of the work of millions of workers, from loggers cutting trees to waitresses serving those same loggers coffee.[57] This is how modern economies work, combining the results of millions industries in a bewilderingly complicated pattern, far beyond the scope of any academic or politician to model and control.

Whatever reasons we may have to plan transport, it can't be importance or complexity alone. Indeed, throughout the nineteenth century, transport grew in its reach, speed and affordability – and all without public control.

Myth Two: Competition in transport is wasteful

> Co-ordination is a blessed word, capable of varying and conflicting interpretations... Applied to the transport problem it may mean the avoidance of unnecessary over lapping of services, or the elimination of uneconomic or even economic competition.
>
> Dr W. H. Coates, 'Report on The Transport Problem in Great Britain'[58]

---

57   Leonard Read, *I, Pencil*, 1958
58   Coates, July 1942

> The logic of the rail industry is that... decisions have to be
> made in the best interests of the railways as a whole, which
> leads to the inevitable conclusion that only a large British-
> Rail type organisation can manage the railways. Only if
> there is a single body which takes overall responsibility for
> the railways will it be possible to regain control over costs
> and run the industry efficiently.
> Christian Wolmar, *Broken Rails* [59]

You only have to look at the history of Britain's transport system to see the waste private companies bring, the
Planners argue. Duplicate train lines where only one would
have done. No co-ordination between different transport
modes, the inventors of the Underground paying no attention to the impact their creation would have on the struggling tram market. Why do we need two trains companies
when all anybody really wants is a single ticket working on
every train? Why should we pay greedy businessman excess
profits, when that money could instead be funnelled back
into greater investment in the network?

Now, economies of scale are a very important force in
economics, and it is for precisely this reason that many of
the early train or bus companies quickly amalgamated into
larger networks, or formed alliances. In the early days of
the railway you often had to buy new tickets for each of
the different small railways you travelled on, and this was
clearly inefficient. We're seeing now the same process in the
air as airlines try to join together into ever bigger coalitions
to offer their customers a wider choice of destination.

But when Planners assume that economies of scale are
always important, that 'bigger is better', they ignore equally
important economic forces that act in the opposite direction. The problem with large organisations, whether in the

59   Wolmar, *On the Wrong Line: How Ideology and Incompetence
      Wrecked Britain's Railways*, 2005, p. 338

public or private sector, is that they find it hard to deal with two other equally crucial ideas in economics: *incentives* and *knowledge*.

Individuals and employees always respond to some set of incentives, although these might not always be the incentives we would like. When two companies merge, the cut-throat competition of market forces is replaced by the intrigue of internal corporate politics and bureaucracy. This is part of the reason why an organisation as massive as British Rail found it hard to innovate. Empirical evidence is beginning to show what most businessmen instinctively know: the cost of increased bureaucracy can often outweigh any efficiencies of scale. Statistically it seems the case that the more employees a company has, the lower the amount of profit per employee.[60]

Knowledge is just as fundamental. We live in an uncertain world, where many complex systems interact with results that are impossible to predict. Knowledge is often unavoidably local – the man working on the rails can see the true situation better than his boss trapped back in central office – but in large organisations, it is often difficult to pass autonomy and responsibility down to those who know the most.

Competition and spare capacity in markets are wasteful if we know precisely what to do in an industry, and can perfectly motivate everyone to work together. But if we don't and we can't, then they are essential. They're the market's means of evolving closer to better serve consumers.

Myth Three: As transport companies are natural monopolies, they should be run by the government

The functions required of transport are too variable, not only with the conditions in different areas, but also with

---

60   http://www.nytimes.com/2010/12/19/magazine/19Urban_West-t.
       html?_r=4&pagewanted=all

the almost infinite variety of goods to be carried and the conditions of the time, even down to the conditions of an individual trader. It follows that the end envisaged cannot be attained by free competition.
Dr W. H. Coates, 'Report on The Transport Problem in Great Britain'[61]

This [capital] requires very large amounts of financial investment; more, in fact, than any single enterprise can be expected to raise. In addition the returns on this investment are likely to be many years in coming and will accrue to the whole community, rather than to individual investors. For this reason these investments are more often and more easily made by governments than by private companies...
Philip Bagwell and Peter Lyth, *Transport in Britain*[62]

The reason that transport doesn't work as free market, the Planners argue, is the huge cost of constructing a new road, railway or airport. Your average person – or even company – can't just raise the funds to create a new transport organisation to take on the market leader. There are huge, in the jargon, 'barriers to entry'. That means that once a company has created its infrastructure, the Planners say, has an effective monopoly. There's no competition. That means the company can keep increasing its prices as much as it likes, and worry little about the quality of the service it provides.

While Planners are right that usually only very large companies can afford to run transport services, this is hardly an unprecedented situation in our economy.

What we normally see in most markets today are effective oligopolies, a couple of corporate giants ruling the market for a decade or so: Microsoft and Google, the BBC and Sky, Coke and Pepsi, Tesco and Sainsbury. The presence

---

61   Coates, July 1942
62   Bagwell & Lyth, 2002 pp. XII–XIII

of a single competitor or two keeps the company honest in the short term, and in the medium term if the corporation becomes lazy there is usually some start-up waiting to take their place. IBM is toppled by Microsoft who in turn is toppled by Google. Of the 100 biggest firms in Britain in 1907, only four still survive today.[63] The average corporation has a lifespan of forty to fifty years.[64] Note that most of these corporate giants are just as dependent on massive investments of capital to grow their economies of scale, and lower their costs. Server farms, global distribution networks and tens of thousands of staff do not come cheaply.

This model doesn't work perfectly. Occasionally some companies in a monopoly position do abuse their position and power.

Fortunately, we already have a set of institutions and procedures for use in such a situation. We have the Competition Commission and competition law, ready and standing by to make sure that large companies are not holding up the progress of a market.

Most industries face barriers to entry, and lack as much competition as we'd like. That doesn't mean markets in them can't work.

Myth Four: Transport needs to be subsidised

Because transport is a public service of some importance, it must provide for some needs which are not fully remunerative.
Dr W. H. Coates, 'Report on The Transport Problem in Great Britain'[65]

---

63   http://ideas.repec.org/p/wso/wpaper/8.html (the four are WH Smith, GKN, Prudential and British American Tobacco)

64   http://www.nytimes.com/2010/12/19/magazine/19Urban_West-t. html?_r=4&pagewanted=all

65   Coates, July 1942

> Whereas the British Government... treated the railways
> as an industry that had to earn a commercial return on
> its capital, France and Germany viewed their railways
> in terms of their benefits to the community at large...
> [Such dedication] to a plan for transport has been almost
> completely lacking in Britain in the twentieth century.
> Philip Bagwell and Peter Lyth, *Transport in Britain*[66]

We all know that transport is hugely important to a society
and its economy. When people and goods can move around
more quickly or more cheaply, they can take advantages
of more opportunities in business and life. The better the
transport networks in a city, the further people can travel in
to get to work. The more people that can get to work, the
wealthier a city as a whole is.

But because these benefits are widely distributed, some
of the extra value created by new transport connections
doesn't go into higher ticket prices and profits, but escapes
away into land values or the additional satisfaction of
customers. In the long term it means companies will have
less incentive to build additional transport links that would
make everyone better off.

This is what economists call a 'positive externality', and
it occurs everywhere.

If your neighbour keeps an especially attractive garden
that puts a smile on your face on the way to work in the
morning, that's a positive externality. If you take a vaccine
that not only stops you from catching some horrible
infectious disease but passing it on, then that's a positive
externality. When a private inventor creates a new idea
that other companies can go on to profit from, then that's a
positive externality as well.

In fact, it's the very ubiquity of these positive externalities that weakens this argument in the case of transport. It

probably isn't practical to go around subsidising people for keeping good-looking gardens. At the same time, we often find that markets provide ample new innovations even when they don't seem to be capturing the full benefit. Gutenberg didn't keep a millionth of the value created by the printing press or John Logie Baird the television, and yet as a society we still ended up with televisions and printing presses.

Does this mean there's never a case for government support in case of positive externalities?

No.

Often we do see an area that is so crucial and under-provided that some government support seems a pragmatic best way forward. Providing funding for basic scientific research is a good example of this, as is government paying for vaccines or nudging you to take them.

What it does mean is that the simple existence of positive externalities on their own is not a blank cheque giving grounds for unlimited support. There are costs as well as benefits to handing out government subsidies, and weighing up the balance between the two is not easy. Subsidies can distort incentives as well as reinforce them, making industries focus their efforts on winning the affection of governments rather than the satisfactions of customers. Worse, once we have started providing an industry with subsidies, it is often difficult to stop.

New transport infrastructure can be essential to an economy, but that doesn't grant it the right to unlimited funds.

Myth Five: Planning is non ideological

The purpose of this Report is to provide a reasoned and dispassionate survey, from a transport and business point of view, and not from any political angle... It ... recommends the adoption of a comprehensive scheme for the

unification, under a public service corporation, of all the
means of internal transport.
Dr W. H. Coates, 'Report on The Transport Problem in
Great Britain'[67]

[Privatisation of the railways] represented one of the
great political and economic crimes of the twentieth
century... Ideology was a crucial factor in the havoc
that ensued.
Christian Wolmar, *Broken Rails*[68]

The problem with the privatisation wave of the 1980s,
Planners complain, is that it was a radical ideologically
motivated attack on systems that had already proved themselves to work.

By contrast, planning is a neutral, rational attempt
to weigh up the costs and benefits of various policies.
Economists, sociologists and environmental scientists can,
after appropriate consultation with the public, draw up a
plan for the best way forward.

It should be obvious – simply from reading over the last
five myths – that this isn't quite correct.

Embedded in many of the Planners' models are assumptions that are, frankly, quasi-Marxist in their outlook.
While they lack the class-war element of a pure socialism, their broad outlook is that of early twentieth century
Progressivism: government taking a strong hand, to push
the country and economy forward, and push out the vagar-
ies and inefficiencies of the market.

Transport planners have their own special interests and
affections, a 'groupthink identity' that defines themselves
against the uninformed masses of society. They are very

---

67 Coates, July 1942
68 Wolmar, *On the Wrong Line: How Ideology and Incompetence
Wrecked Britain's Railways*, 2005 p. 329

concerned about public transport, and think we should be using far more of it. They believe focusing on concerns of profit and competition is to completely fail to understand the sector.

Most of all they are angry about what they see as our society's obsession with the automobile. They believe that cars are bad for the environment, spewing out carbon dioxide and poisonous gases. They argue that they are dangerous, leading to thousands of preventable deaths a year. Moreover, they believe they're bad for the economy, with too few people understanding the extent to which cars are subsidised in our society.

To the Planners, the worst crime of the car is that it creates a suburban, atomised culture is frankly, well, *American*.

It would be a mistake to throw aside completely the Planners' concerns. They have a point in that there are often implicit subsidies towards cars that we need to consider. Cars do indeed have bad effects on safety and the environment.

But once we have taken those factors into account, we have no greater right to tell people what method of transport to use than what type of film they ought to watch. By trying to control the way the population lives, the Planners have made it harder for the public to take their serious recommendations seriously.

Where Planning Goes Wrong
The dream of planning was that it would create a more integrated, efficient system. The reality is that it has slowed innovation, increased waste and caused umpteen unintended consequences.

In the next section, we will look at the Planners' attempts to bring order to the transport sector: planning how much capacity we'll need, how we'll move away from fossil fuels, solve the problems caused by transport monopolies, work out which new infrastructure projects to build or ensure our safety. As we'll see, despite starting from often good intentions, their planning has either failed to deliver or ironically made things far worse.

We started this section with an overview of the caricatures that sometimes get passed on about free market economics, and we should be careful not to commit the reverse sin and pass on a stereotype about the planning process.

Planning, as the word suggests, is essential, even if plans themselves are useless. It really is helpful for a country to think hard about what sort of infrastructure it will need in future, to look at the best and most efficient way to transition to a greener economy, to ensure new developments are in the best interests of all, and to minimise whenever possible needless waste of human life.

The problem arises when we take this planning too far, putting more weight on the predictions of academic models than they can bear. Models are a guide to what might happen – our best guess. They cannot be taken as the last word on the subject, for now and eternity.

Often, it is not so much what models contain, as what they completely miss out. No Victorian transport modeller could see how the rise of the steam engine would completely change the landscape of the country. No Edwardian would have guessed how quickly the car would take the train's place. As late as the 1980s, few would have foreseen the imminent rise of the budget airlines, expanding the possibility of cheap aviation to all.

In the 1940s, at the height of the intellectual mania for the big state, it is no surprise that Planners thought transport could only prosper under their control. In today's world, where we have a more nuanced view of the relative strength of markets and governments, we should not be so quick to repeat their mistakes.

PART TWO

THE WRONG TURN

ECONOMY

Forget the threat of Peak Oil. Many argue the latest phenomenon is Peak Travel.

For the last two hundred years we've sought to travel ever further in our daily commute or annual holiday, but it is possible, after all, to have too much of a good thing. There is only so much of our day we want to spend confined to a car or train. What has truly transformed global politics and economics in the last hundred years are not the changes in transport, but changes in the technology of communications. The future of the economy seems to be based on stationary services, not the heavy goods and freight of manufacturing. Perhaps the age of surging transport investment has come to an end?

Indeed, there is evidence across the Western world that demand for transport is now reaching a plateau. Statisticians have looked at what are known as total vehicle miles travelled in the US, Canada, Japan, Sweden, Australia, and the UK. Across all these countries, the distances travelled seem not just to be levelling off, but falling.[69]

The reasons for this fall, the researchers themselves admit, remain unclear. The fall seems clearest in the miles we drive. Other means of travel, such as international flights or rail journeys in the UK, continue to grow. The fact that the slowdown is occurring across the Western world suggests that this isn't a result of any particular government policy. The slowdown seems to pre-date both the recent rises in the oil price and the financial crisis.[70]

---

69 Millard-Ball & Schipper, 2010
70 UCLA Transport Scholar Eric A. Morris has a highly useful series of blog posts on the topic starting at:

When superseded in the past, old methods of transport such as the canal or horse-driven buggy saw drastic rates of decline. As the modern economy brings people closer together in larger cities, perhaps cars have at last reached the end of their dominance.

If this represents more than a short-term statistical quirk, it will clearly have a huge impact on the future needs of transport. We will move from an era of transport growth to one of consolidation.

The leading paradigm for transport policy in the last sixty years has been something known as 'predict-and-provide'. Expert Planners have carefully watched the social and economic trends taking place in the country, and tried to work out exactly how many roads, railways and runways are required for the coming decades.

As we will see, this method has been far from an unqualified success. It is difficult to argue convincingly that Britain currently enjoys adequate investment in transport. Our roads are congested, our airports are full and we have constantly to pump ever more money into the railways to keep up with demand. Planners have failed to foresee every significant change, from the revival of rail to the increasing popularity of London.

However, if there is less demand for transport in the future, then perhaps it doesn't matter if predict-and-provide doesn't work. We can make do with the roads we already have. There would be no need for any new runways in the south-east of the country and we can instead focus on 'better, not bigger' airports.[71] Why bother to build expensive new investments, such as High

---

http://www.freakonomicsmedia.com/2011/02/07/whats-putting-the-brakes-on-the-growth-of-driving/

71   The new coalition government has promised 'bigger, not better airports' as part of their policy alternative to a third runway at Heathrow.

Speed Rail, if we will all be more than satisfied with video conferencing instead?

Why is Traffic Demand Slowing Down?

So, what has caused the slowdown in demand for transport across the world?

Economic theory seems to suggest there should be a limit to demand. At the most basic level, greater mobility is beneficial to businesses and citizens as it allows a wider range of choice. If you can drive, you no longer have to put up with the selection of the village shop but can travel to the local supermarket.

However, there is clearly a limit to this. Upgrading to a supermarket may be worth a half-hour drive, but most people don't feel it is always worth travelling a still further hour to the nearby superstore. There are diminishing returns to choice, and thus in turn transport as well.

There have been many reasons to travel further in recent decades. The advent of cheap cars has given us freedom to roam further in pursuit of our daily errands. We live in smaller households, making it harder to share vehicles. Modern tourism has allowed more people to holiday abroad. Perhaps most significant of all, the introduction of women into the workforce has doubled the number of people struggling to make their daily commute.

These trends all seem to be coming to an end. The Western world (and America, in particular) is car saturated – everyone who wants a vehicle already has one. The Green Belt has stopped the expansion of our cities and therefore halted the lengthening of the commute into the office. In 1950, around 34 per cent of women over sixteen worked, whereas the proportion has now stabilised at about 60 per cent.[72]

---

72   http://www.freakonomicsmedia.com/2011/02/07/whats-putting-the-brakes-on-the-growth-of-driving/

A more worrying possibility is that underlying demand hasn't gone away so much as become frustrated by the stagnation in supply. As car ownership exploded in the mid twentieth century, governments did their best to accommodate it with ambitious programmes of road building. They developed new highways and motorways to link up the edges of their countries. After the completion of these initial motorway networks, public development of roads large stopped or slowed to a crawl. Even before the end of major construction in 1995, miles constructed significantly lagged behind miles travelled. Between 1980 and 2005, the country saw an 80 per cent increase in traffic, but only 10 per cent more capacity.[73] The inevitable result was that our roads became more congested.

It may be the case that we are not driving more because the increase in traffic congestion means that it is no longer worth it. We would rather stay at home than put up with another hour trapped in a traffic jam.

One of the most intriguing findings of transport researchers is that humans are surprisingly predictable in their commuting tastes. When left to their own devices most people seem to allocate around one hour for their daily travel time – half an hour there to work, and half an hour back. Commuters in as diverse settings as the West, Latin America, Asia, communist East Europe and even African villages gravitated towards an average travelling times of one and a half hours. [74] This statistical trend seems to be so stable that some even hypothesise it is the result of an innate human time budget allocated on travel.

The speed that our vehicles travel has not drastically increased in the last few decades. In many cases it has even slowed as increased congestion makes it harder to get

---

73   http://www.guardian.co.uk/society/2005/oct/26/epublic.
     technology12
74   Schafer, 2000

around. If both the average speeds and the time we spend travelling stay the same, then clearly we should expect to see a stable distance travelled as well.

Unless we see a reduction in congestion in the coming years or improved technology, we shouldn't expect to see much movement in this level of demand.

The Local Economy

Some commentators go even further: not only will travel demand level off in the future, it will fall.

Ever more of our daily life will be subsumed into the digital arena, these commentators argue, while concerns over climate change will force us to create a far more locally focused economy. Workers in the future will spend their time building web sites, rather than cars or toys. Even if it were convenient to maintain our current globetrotting lifestyles, aviation will become increasingly unaffordable, economically and environmentally.

But for all the convenience of digital technologies, talking to a monitor is never going to be a substitute for meeting someone face to face. While our economy is now dominated by services, many of these services are in turn traded for physical goods from abroad. It is worth remembering that despite concerns about the decline of manufacturing employment in Britain, the absolute level of manufacturing output has increased. While we may consume relatively fewer physical goods than services, it is another, more heroic assumption altogether to believe that the absolute volume will go down.

The benefits of a locally sourced economy are often overstated. Transport is usually only a minority contribution to the energy cost of producing any particular good. It is far more efficient to grow wine in naturally temperate climates and ship it across the world than to try and artificially replace an environment here.

As many totalitarian states have discovered, an obsession with a local economy and self sufficiency is as often the route to poverty as wealth. In a recent experiment, Kelly Cobb of Drexel University found that trying to source a cheap suit from materials within a 100-mile radius multiplied its cost by a factor of a hundred.[75] We will need more transport and trade to support our growing wealth, not less.

The prevalence of the digital economy seems ironically to have placed a greater value on real life experiences. The price for musical gigs and live performances continues to increase as people seek experiences unmediated by an electronic screen.

The economic story of the twentieth century has been the rise of globalisation. There seems no reason to expect that trend to reverse.

How Much Transport Will We Need in the Future?

So what will happen to our transport demand in the future? Are the 'peak travel' theorists right that demand will stop increasing in the future?

There are reasons to be sceptical. It is not inevitable that transport should peak. Food production, for example, continues to rise, even though we long ago may have reached the point of diminishing returns. Then again, it is easy to be wasteful with extraneous food, for it only requires more money. Transport also takes up our time, the one quantity perhaps we still never have enough of.

Moreover, in the past commentators have all been too keen to claim that some mode of transport has 'peaked', when a few years later growth has resumed as relentlessly as ever. Green commentators have claimed that demand for aviation is going away,[76] or the government that cities such as London have reached a 'mature' state of development,

---

75   Ridley, 2010, p. 55
76   http://www.guardian.co.uk/environment/georgemonbiot/2009/
     may/22/ba-heathrow-airlines-recession

and so there is no need for new investment. In both cases, demand returned as soon as we left economic recession.

In the short term, transport demand is very closely linked to the state of the economic cycle – the richer we feel, the more we travel for business or pleasure. Only in long-term statistics can we really tell whether our demand for transport is going up or down. While our current evidence for 'peak travel' goes back ten years,[77] it is best, after all, to require significant evidence to accept the end of a century-long trend.

As the country grows richer, we would expect that its citizens would want to spend some of that wealth on travelling further and more frequently. Even today, transport remains unequally distributed. The wealthy are far more likely not just to enjoy a summer holiday, but frequent business trips and the occasional weekend break. Allowing more people to enjoy the benefits of travel is a progressive goal.

We simply don't know what will happen to transport demand in decades from now, and we should be sceptical of anyone who argues otherwise. It may be that we see a divergence between transport modes as travel in the air and on rail continues to grow, while traffic on the roads stays at current levels. Or perhaps not much will depend on the future path of technology and politics. This is not a situation we can plan.

But despite our inability to predict future demand, we can be sure of a more important point – we will need more investment in our transport supply all the same.

The Importance of Transport
The methods of transport we can use have always enormously mattered for the way we live and the kind of work we can do.

Better transport links make it easier for different areas to trade. More trade means that different areas can special-

77   Millard-Ball & Schipper, 2010

ise in the particular industries and skills to which they are best suited. The good transport links of the Roman Empire allowed Rome to feed on grain from Spain and Egypt.[78] When the Empire broke down, and its roads went with it, the whole of Western Europe became poorer. The economist Paul Krugman has argued that the introduction of the railway in the nineteenth century allowed America to differentiate into a farm belt in the south and manufacturing belt in the north.[79]

In the twentieth century, the most important advance for transport was perhaps not the aeroplane or the space rocket, but the containers used on freight ships. Despite being little more than a glorified metal box, the standardised dimensions of containers allowed goods to be moved across the planet much more easily, helping inaugurate the current age of globalisation. Together with technological advances they have helped cut the costs of transporting goods by 90 per cent in the last hundred years.[80]

By contrast, the costs of transporting people have not declined to anywhere near the same extent. In many cases, the monetary and time costs are even going up as increased congestion slows down the roads. These effects are at their worst in the heart of the world's cities.

People behave differently in cities. They're more productive and more sociable. They produce more patents, and commit more crimes. Cities meld cultures, industries and people together in a way that is hard to replicate anywhere else. No other part of Britain can match London in its art, theatre, music or social scene. 'When a man is tired of London he is tired of life,' as Dr Johnson said.

---

78   Glaesar, 2011, p. 168
79   Krugman, 2009
80   Glaeser, Edward L. and J. E. Kohlhase. 'Cities, Regions and the Decline of Transport Costs.' Papers in Regional Science 83, 1 (2004): 197–228.

But the advantages to city life turn out to be more than
cultural. In the old economy, the strongholds of a country's
wealth used to be its industrial cities: the textile mills of the
North or the car companies in Detroit. These days, in our
service-based economy, the factory has lost its importance.
Instead, our prosperity depends on the workers themselves.

Born in Somerset, US physicist Geoffrey West decided to
leave behind his lifetime work of theoretical particle physics after Congress cancelled the funding for a new supercol-
lider particle accelerator in 1993. Instead, he applied his
keen intellect and strong work ethic (he claims never to
eat lunch) to other problems in the sciences. For example,
working with ecologist Jim Brown, he found a remarkably
consistent relationship between the average size of a species
and its metabolic rate or blood pressure.[81]

Recently, he has turned his attention to the human world,
to see if he could uncover similar regularities in companies and
cities. After two years of collecting data, he believes that he has
indeed found such patterns that reoccur every time humans
cluster together. Given the population of a metropolitan area,
he claims to be able to predict to 85 per cent accuracy, 'its
average income and the dimensions of its sewer system.'[82]

More than half the world's population now lives in
cities, with an extra five million joining them each month.[83]
The reason for this, West claims, is that the interactions
that cities make possible amplify the productivity of each
individual living within them. If you double the size of a
city, each person working in it becomes 15 per cent more
productive. The closer we pack together knowledge workers, the easier they find it to mingle and network, find jobs
or do business. Indeed, West's data suggests that nearly

---

81   http://www.time.com/time/magazine/article/0,9171,1187290,00.html
82   http://www.nytimes.com/2010/12/19/magazine/19Urban_West-t.
      html?_r=2
83   Glaesar, 2011, p. 1

all socioeconomic variables in a city increase by about 15 percent: economic activity, construction, bank deposits, traffic, crime, even disease.[84]

Instinctively we feel that cities must be bad for the environment, but first impressions can be misleading. It is true that cities are noisy, grimy and dominated by concrete. However, by packing people ever closer together, individuals and families living in cities can get by using far less energy than their countryside counterparts. One of the greenest actions a city planner can approve is the construction of a new skyscraper. According to urban economist Edward Glaesar, 'the average single-family detached home [in America] consumes 88 per cent more electricity than the average apartment in a five-or-more-unit building... [Overall] a household in San Francisco emits 60 per cent less carbon than its equivalent in Memphis.'[85]

Despite the more efficient nature of cities, we've often held them back in the past with zoning requirements or restrictions on the heights of buildings. Many of these regulations were put in place by transport planners, and their close cousins, urban planners, seeking to create their own vision of what a modern society should look like. While nobody wants to see the tearing down of our historical architecture, we have to avoid becoming overly protective of urban areas and seeking to freeze them in development. This can have huge economic consequences – statistics show that Greater London is more than 50 per cent more productive than the rest of the UK.[86] The more people we can comfortably fit into the city, the wealthier our country becomes.

---

84   http://www.nytimes.com/2010/12/19/magazine/19Urban_West-t.html?_r=2

85   Glaesar, 2011, pp. 209–210

86   http://www.ft.com/cms/s/0/d6074404-48f5-11e0-af8c-00144feab49a.html#axzz1G63J9QYT

At present, the tide of government opinion seems to be shifting towards deregulation and the removal of urban plans. This will only put more pressure on transport, the other factor holding back the development of cities. If people can't easily move around a city, it is difficult to live or work in it.

The current capacity both within and between our cities is nearly full up. If demand does continue to rise, the inevitable result will either be people forced away or more congestion and queuing. It's worth remembering that congestion isn't just frustrating and a waste of time, but is of itself a huge cost to the economy. A business executive stuck in a traffic jam is a business executive not generating any economic value.

Connections between cities matter as well. The size, strength and function of cities have always depended heavily on their transport links. In the past, cities such as Liverpool and New York have gained from their access to the oceans while London and Chicago gained from their access to inward waters.

When an international business is trying to choose which country to invest in, the quality of transport links both within major cities and out to the rest of the world clearly matters. The UK is lucky in the advantages it currently enjoys from its language and time zone, but few businesses would locate here for the transport system. The World Bank among others has complained that infrastructure remains inadequate and should be a significant priority for investment.[87] According to the CBI, 70 per cent of senior business figures judged UK infrastructure to be poor and 85 per cent agreed that this had an impact on their decision to invest. Sixty-one per cent of firms believed that the provision of roads was getting worse.[88]

---

87 Going for Growth, OECD, 2010, p. 150

88 Helm, Wardlaw, & Caldecott, Delivering a 21st Century Infrastructure for Britain, 2009, p. 6

Opinions differ as to how we reached this position. Left-wing commentators argue that the UK's crumbling transport is a consequence of Britain's mania for laissez-faire and a short-termist Treasury that refused to invest. In contrast, they argue, the Continent has historically understood the benefits of greater co-ordination and enjoyed a political settlement that accepted transport networks should not aim solely at making a profit.

It's not clear that this is true. In the nineteenth century, the private-sector-led UK and US railways remained throughout the century easily the most advanced in the world. From 1800 to 1830, the construction of private sector turnpike roads cost around 6.2 per cent of the New England and Middle Atlantic states 1830 GDP. By contrast, a hundred years later, construction of the US highways between 1956 and 1995 took up only 4.3 per cent of 1996 GDP.[89]

Nevertheless, whatever your ideological standpoint, the stark fact is that UK investment has lagged behind its competitors. As recently as the late 1990s, investment in the UK as a proportion of GDP remained only 1.39 per cent compared to an OECD average of 3.14 per cent. It increased to 1.77 per cent of GDP from 2004, but still badly lagged behind the OECD's 3.13 per cent. The think tank Policy Exchange recently calculated what it believed to be the minimum level of adequate investment in UK infrastructure – a colossal £434 billion in total, with £120 billion of investment needed in transport alone.[90]

This record of underinvestment has left the country with a railway optimised for Victorian times and a motorway network barely updated since its construction forty years ago. Only 30 per cent of UK railways are electrified,

---

89 Winston, 2010, p. 2

90 Helm, Wardlaw, & Caldecott, Delivering a 21st Century Infrastructure for Britain, 2009

compared to more than 70 per cent in Belgium, Sweden and the Netherlands. China has already constructed a motorway network ten times the size of the UK's, and the UK has a shorter road length per person than any other major country. Spain, France and Germany each have motorway networks more than twice the size of the UK's.[91]

One of the reasons we should seek to expand this is that new transport investment can often pay for itself by the increases it makes to economic efficiency. But perhaps more importantly, if we choose to do nothing congestion and delay will steadily increase on their own.

The UK's population is predicted to grow steadily. Even if the average person never wished to travel more than they do today, transport demanded by the population as a whole will continue to rise. The Office for National Statistics predicts that Britain will have an extra sixteen million people by 2050. This is the equivalent of adding an extra two cities, both as large as London.[92] All of these additional people will want to use roads, railways and airports as well.

A static demand and population wouldn't necessarily imply that we didn't need any more investment either. Total demand can stay still as the distribution of people within a country shifts from economic forces changing the nature of its industries. Britain's population is gradually moving southwards, and towards the city.

And even if we believe this migration won't have a big effect, that doesn't mean we will want to settle for the same transport technologies tomorrow as we do today. It is a sad indicator of the lack of recent technological progress in transport that we simply accept that we will be using roughly the same sort of roads, trains or aeroplanes thirty years from now as we do today.

---

91 Wellings & Lipson, 2008, p. 8

92 http://www.optimumpopulation.org/opt.more.ukpoptable.html

If, as most experts and commentators predict, we have to move transport away from fossil fuels and onto zero carbon technologies, we will need high levels of investment. We will need new electric charging networks across our roads and to electrify the remaining railways. The magnitude of such a change could be as big as the introduction of the car itself.

Predict-and-provide rarely works well. Given its questionable record over the twentieth century, we should not be too quick to accept the biggest prediction of all, that transport demand has come to a halt. The last things we need are inflexible plans based on abstract models of the state of the nation three decades from now. Nobody can safely predict that far into the future, just as nobody could have foreseen the rise of mass tourism or the arrival of the car. Neither is it a good idea to spend money for the sake of it, increasing our expenditure to improve our position in some league table. Britain doesn't need its own collection of Alaskan-style 'bridges to nowhere'.

But despite the uncertainty of the future, the safest assumption has to be that population and climate pressures will force us to invest more in our transport infrastructure. If we don't want to be left behind in the global economy, we will have to do better. The state of Britain's infrastructure means that we need not only more trains, but roads, runways and tube lines too.

ENVIRONMENT

If the threat to the environment is the greatest challenge we face in the future, then perhaps, as Green MP Caroline Lucas suggests, we need to restore the same spirit that allowed us to overcome our greatest challenge in the past. What is needed is the determination of wartime Britain, in which the entire population accepted in a spirit of communal sacrifice that economic wellbeing was not the greatest priority.

In January 2011 the Green Party launched a report, *The New Home Front,* looking at the inspiration Britain could draw from the last world war. 'If we are to overcome [the threat of climate change],' Lucas argues, '... then we need to mobilise as a nation in a way we haven't seen since 1945.'[93]

In the war motor fuel was strictly rationed, making it difficult to drive. *The New Home Front* approvingly records that 'Between 1938 and 1944 there was a 95 per cent drop in use of motor vehicles' while 'public transport use increased 13 per cent from 1938–1943'.[94] Flying on a plane was of course an impossibility. Passengers were asked only to travel by train if their journey was really essential. According to Lucas, 'Wartime slogans such as "Is your journey really necessary?" remain relevant today, when so much business travel could be replaced by video conferencing.'[95]

---

93   http://www.guardian.co.uk/environment/blog/2011/jan/20/
      home-front-war-climate-change

94   Simms, 2011, p. 10

95   http://www.guardian.co.uk/environment/blog/2011/jan/20/
      home-front-war-climate-change

Today, while few strictly weigh up the carbon pros and cons of our railway trips, the message is beginning to resonate with ordinary Britons. Few can book their annual holiday to Spain without feeling a little guilty, and wondering if they should plant a tree as a carbon offset. Most at least try to cut down on frivolous trips in the car, although might admit, if pushed, that they do less than they should.

After all, we have often been told of the frightening truth of where our selfish carbon consumption will lead. The world will see melted ice caps, flooded low-lying countries and millions of new refugees pouring out of developed countries. Ecosystems will be devastated, and thousands of species doomed to extinction. The possibility exists of complete breakdown of global climate patterns, leading to the end of civilisation as we know it.

Compared to this nightmare, what price a weekend break to Vienna on Easyjet?

It seems that no matter its importance to the economy, Britain simply can't afford any more transport. We have to place strict limits on the numbers of planes flying from our airports, or the cars on our roads. We need as quickly as possible to transition the population from private to public transport, and invest as much money as we can into new green technologies. Only extreme measures can save us from environmental catastrophe.

For the Planners, the environment acts as the primary motivation for their struggle to make us give up our cars and trips abroad. Their long campaign against the two 'dirty' form of transports has won real achievements. Governments of all persuasions have largely given up on extensive programmes of road building. It is now government policy that no new runways should be built in the south-east of England, even though demand is expected to double.[96]

---

96   The Future of Air Transport White Paper, 2003

But, surprisingly, it turns out that none of these unpleasant predictions are true. There is no need for a new generation of Planners to dictate what transport we can and can't use. Cars need not be the environmental catastrophe that Planners pretend. Indeed, you can keep your foreign holiday, and save the environment at the same time.

The Carbon Diet

Environmental activists despair: humanity is too selfish to ever cut emissions of its own accord. What is needed is a completely new type of society and economy where protecting the environment becomes our first priority. All other objectives, such as economic growth or tackling poverty, will have to be subordinated to this primary task.

But even if this were true, turning the struggle against climate change into a moral crusade is unlikely to be effective.

Most of us struggle with the far simpler task of looking after our own health, let alone the condition of the planet. Even if we could maintain more self control with carbon than most of us manage with carbs, how can we possibly work out what choices we should make? Few of us have any notion how to calculate the true carbon cost of the goods we buy or the transport we use. How could we possibly add up all the links in the supply chain, or know exactly how the energy was generated?

While using moralistic language may have some virtues for the short term, these virtues are easily outweighed by its flaws. Stigmatising the fat has not helped stop the obesity epidemic. Stigmatising carbon is unlikely to stop package holidays.

Behavioural change is very difficult. Whether it be changing diet, starting a new exercise regime or keeping to a budget, most of us have some experience of the difficulties of self-control. These struggles only become harder when the gains are far off. They become exponentially more difficult still when the gains accrue to people in foreign counties who may not even be born yet.

Worse than just being ineffective, hyperbolic moral rhetoric can actually make it harder for us to cut back on carbon.

By turning carbon into an ideological evil, we summon up the worst of our reactionary instincts. Some have gone so far as to turn the environmentalist cause into a religious belief in Gaia, and against civilisation itself, in which all new development is a threat. No new road is complete without the sight of activists chaining themselves to trees, airports have got used to groups such as Greenpeace and Plane Stupid breaking in, and even the railways, long the favourite of the environmental movement, are now facing fierce resistance against the new High Speed 2 (HS2)railway line.

While such protests may be effective in polarising debate and even stopping developments in the short term, they are unlikely to add up to a coherent strategy. It is not abstaining from one chocolate bar that makes a difference, but putting in place a sustainable lifestyle. Short-term starvation is all too often followed by guilty gorging later.

To start with, it is helpful to put some numbers into the debate and get a sense of the scale of the problem. It turns out that the impact of transport on the environment is hardly as overwhelming as the environmentalist fixation on the sector might suggest. Government figures suggest that only 21 per cent of the economy's carbon is produced by transport.

The focus on aviation in particular looks unfair, as only 21 per cent of the carbon produced by transport in turn comes from aeroplanes. By contrast, an overwhelming 43 per cent of transport's carbon emissions is produced by passenger cars and a further 13 per cent from heavy goods vehicles.[97] Much of the government's target for a reduction in carbon of 80 per cent by 2050 could be met by

---

97   Department for Transport, 2011, p. 20

changing the source of power of these vehicles from gasoline to carbon-free electricity.

In other words, the problem we face is a problem not of changing our lifestyles, but changing our technology. Moral exhortations are not going to speed up the development of lithium-ion batteries to drive our cars, or new biofuels to power our planes. Any real moral worldview would have to take into account the effects on the poor in the developing world of holding back our economy.

But this isn't grounds for complacency. The world's transport systems won't move away from fossil fuels automatically. Gasoline powered cars are as popular as ever, and there remains a real fear that while aviation may be a minimal contributor to carbon at present, it will rapidly grow in size in the next fifty years.

We need some sort of strategy to ease our transport off its current addiction to fossil fuels.

The Plan to Save the World

Perhaps the best way forward is our old friend planning.

Just as in war when the government rationed our food and clothes, now it could ration carbon for us. The Planners can take a careful look at what facilities society needs to function and, through a careful programme of regulation and subsidies, move our economy and infrastructure to a carbon-free future. In areas where carbon-free technology seems implausible, such as aviation, the government can set tight limits on the numbers allowed. We all know that the future will be dominated by wind farms and electric cars, so why not tilt the rules of the game and speed things up?

This, more or less, is the current government programme. The government has already introduced an exhaustingly long list of measures: sponsoring and supporting railways no matter the costs, taxing cars off the road, restricting growth of airports, subsidising renewable energy and taxing fossil fuels, building a new network for electric cars, moving to a new European Trading System of international carbon trading, and starting a new Green Investment bank.

But while these methods are guaranteed to be expensive, it is far from clear that they will actually solve the problem. Indeed, many Planners agree, believing that they need still *more* power and control to save society from itself.

Already we are beginning to see the idea that the future path of the economy should be carefully planned out, the government setting out a carbon budget just as now it budgets finances. At first, it is supposed, the government should set what path of carbon reduction it wishes to achieve. Then, each sector in turn will be allocated the level of carbon reductions it will be expected to achieve. So, for example, we may wish to reduce the level of carbon emissions in the economy as a whole by say 80 per cent by 2050. Perhaps transport is granted some reprieve, and told it must only reduce its own emissions in turn by 70 per cent.

The targets then get more granular. The Department for Transport can allocate these reductions between transport modes: say 80 per cent cuts for cars, 90 per cent cuts for rail and 50 per cent cuts in aviation. Within the aviation target, the Department can then run its own demand models, and conclude that there is no way to meet its allocated 50 per cent carbon cut without immediately limiting flights from the fastest growing airports.

But this is no way to drive innovation, or keep costs low in an uncertain world. It centralises responsibility and gives control to the political bureaucracy, while it assumes no changes from innovation in the future.

Planning to save the environment suffers all the problems of planning in general.

To start with, it really does matter that we preserve the ability of individuals to make their own choices. To some Planners, there is no reason why they should not tell you what and when you should drive, where your food should be grown, from which countries you may import your clothes, and how many foreign holidays you may take per year.

But we all have different tastes. There is no 'one size fits all' transport solution. The needs of the pensioner in a remote country village and the executive trying to commute into a busy city will obviously be different. Most people accept that they can't always have everything, but they value the option to decide on their own sacrifices. If, given the chance, some would prefer to use their carbon allowance on a foreign holiday, others might be more interested in a vintage car.

Another crucial difficulty is that it is impossible ever to make a plan long, detailed or certain enough to manage such a momentous change. Even if the big strategic choices we should take were clear, there are still tens of thousands of micro-decisions which are far from obvious. Working out all the details, fixing the kinks and then working out how new methods can be applied is very difficult.

Experience suggests that central planning is very bad at technological innovation. Even dynamic tech companies such as Google or Facebook often find it easier to buy outside start-ups than develop new ideas in house. There is little room for trial and error inside a massive bureaucracy, meaning that costs can quickly spiral out of control with minimal benefit at the end.

Planning is unable to deal with choice, uncertainty and the inevitable tradeoffs that new opportunities and dangers offer.

The Trade offs of Climate Change

Global warming is important. The overwhelming scientific consensus suggests our current rate of carbon emissions present a severe ecological and economic threat. Moreover, this harm will overwhelmingly affect those poorest countries who can afford the disturbance least, and there remains an (admittedly) slim chance of apocalyptic catastrophe, which would make all other considerations redundant.

But, on the other hand, there are costs to reducing carbon too. One of the problems with treating climate change as a moral crusade is that it stops us from looking at the costs of our decisions.

Carbon by itself is not 'bad'. If the world economy stopped emitting carbon tomorrow, then significant amounts would still be produced by the natural world. The question in every case is whether the benefit of the carbon is worth the cost and risk it adds to the environment.

In some cases the answer will be unambiguously yes. In other cases – driving an SUV through congested city streets – the answer will be less clear.

Unless we really are running the risk of an apocalyptic situation, then there will inevitably be significant losses from trying to reduce our carbon emissions too far too fast.

Growth is good. It brings us wealth, happiness, health and greater freedom. This used to be uncontroversial, but there exists today an influential lobby who believes that growth should stop altogether. Their motivations are diverse: partly an old fashioned anti-capitalist rhetoric, partly a misreading of the latest research on the relationship between happiness and growth, but most of all an ever growing deep green environmentalism.[98]

This lobby has become one of the transport sector's fiercest enemies. It is happy to attack and stand in any way of each and every new road or runway. If you don't believe in growth in the first place, then, of course, the costs to the economy from giving up development are irrelevant.

---

98 It is a common misconception in today's debate that happiness research has shown there to be no link between happiness and growth for first world countries, but this is misleading. See *Economic Growth and Subjective Well-Being: Reassessing the Easterlin Paradox*, Justin Wolfers & Betty Stevenson, 2008

But away from such extreme views, we do need to take account of growth as the proven route to improving human welfare. The fact that a new runway or motorway will aid growth and the economy is not an all trumping consideration, but it is worth weighing strongly in the balance.

Our goal should be to reduce the maximum amount of carbon emissions with the minimal effect on human welfare. Whenever we're talking about maximising efficiency, what we're really looking at it opportunity for markets.

When Markets Go Wrong

'Climate change presents a unique challenge for economics: it is the greatest and widest-ranging market failure ever seen.'[99] So announced the introduction to the authoritative Stern Review on the problems the world faced from climate change. But if climate change is just another example of a market failure, albeit a particularly momentous and complex case, it is worth looking at the tools we've devised in other cases to handle such problems in the past.

As most of us are at least dimly aware, the way markets are supposed to work is that price rises and falls until demand is equal to supply. However, whenever someone doesn't pay the full cost of their actions, they tend to consume more of a resource than society as a whole can afford.

Let's look at the example of driving.[100] You've already paid a fair amount for the car, and even more on an ongoing basis for your petrol – so what exactly could be the problem?

The problem is that, yes, you have in fact compensated the car manufacturer for the production of the car, and the

---

99   Treasury, 2006
100 For simplicity, we're assuming away the way the actual tax system works here. There is some debate over whether current taxes amount to more or less than the externalities produced by driving.

garage for the sourcing of the petrol. In those cases, you and society are even, and market forces have pretty much worked as we would like them to.

But there are other factors you haven't compensated society for. You haven't paid society for the cost of the carbon you're emitting into the atmosphere, and the global warming this produces. You haven't paid society for the road space your car is taking up, leading to increased congestion and slower driving times for all. What is more, every driver on the road increases the risks of accidents and injury – yet another cost to society.

In other words, you're getting driving on the cheap. If this only affected one person the impact would be small, but repeated across society it leaves us with congested roads, excess pollution and lives lost needlessly.

What is needed is to introduce a new pricing mechanism which adjusts the price so that every individual pays the full cost of their decisions.

So, for example, the government can add an extra charge to your petrol bill to cover the pollution. The government could introduce road pricing, charging you varying amounts for different roads at different times. Theoretically, we could even tax you more if you insisted on not doing up your seatbelt or wearing a motorcycle helmet.

Now, even with all these new charges you may decide your journey is still worth going ahead with. At least now, however, you won't leave the rest of us paying for it.

This isn't a foolproof method. Often the difficulties and impracticalities of fees outweigh any efficiency gains. Before the advent of GPS, it probably would have been more hassle than it was worth to charge individually each driver on every country road. The government shouldn't try to 'nickel and dime' you for everything.

On other occasions, other incentives may be more appropriate or effective than financial ones. Cultural norms can be far more important to us than monetary penalties. It is far from clear, for example, that we wouldn't gain better results by taxing drink driving rather than criminalising it.

But within limits, prices are incredibly powerful tools that are often underused by governments. Often what at first seem intensely complex problems can be solved with nothing other than a simple tax.

Using a Carbon Tax

Exactly the same logic applies to the problem of carbon change across the economy. Fundamentally, the task of rationing the supply of carbon in the economy is no different from the task of rationing the supply of bread.

The virtue of markets is that they allow us to effectively assign millions of micro decisions, giving control to the person in the best position to make the decision. They are open minded, willing to try any method that can reach their goal. Even better, they are flexible enough to take account of individuals' own preferences while still keeping us on track for our ultimate objective.

In our quest to overcome climate change, we want to use incentives and local knowledge, so that everybody in society can play his or her part in reducing carbon. We need new inventors and entrepreneurs to be able to take risks with bold projects, without having first having to get permission from some monolithic bureaucracy. We care about the goal of a safe, clean world but we're not so concerned with how we get there. Set free from an official strategy, inventors are likely to devise many ideas that we could never predict beforehand, whether it be trying to change the climate or devise new forms of transport.

There will be literally millions of decisions that need to be made over the coming decades, but government planners only need to concern themselves about two: what levels of carbon do we wish to have in the economy, and what price do we need to place on carbon to ensure these levels?

These are far from easy questions, and debate continues to rage about the answers. The appropriate price depends heavily on what assumptions you make about both climate science and philosophical questions about how much you value the interests of future generations as against the interests of today.

As good figures as any are those generated by the recent Stern Report.[101] It suggested that to avoid the worst effects of climate change we should seek to limit increases in temperature to a maximum of two degrees centigrade. To achieve this would require stabilising the concentration of carbon in the atmosphere to 550 parts per million. This, in turn, the report concluded, implies that the cost of carbon to the world at large is around $85 per ton CO_2.

In other words, to tackle climate change we need simply to add a carbon tax at this level. For every ton of CO_2 your factory, power station or aeroplane emits you send the taxman an additional cheque for $85. This, noticeably, is a lower level than the taxes we already pay on petrol and aviation.[102] Indeed, the UK already charges a very high tax level on petrol, making up around two-thirds of its cost – and meaning that prices are near double those experienced in the US.[103]

But perhaps $85 is too low. One of the best parts of using a market system is that it remains relatively flexible and open to change later. If the risks to climate later turn out to

---

101   The Stern Report is generally criticised in both directions – for having far too low an estimate of the risk from climate change, and for having far too low a discount rate. The general principles in this text more or flow no matter what numbers the international community decides on – and for the record, Stern's estimate of the cost is near the high end of mainstream valuations.

102   Worstall, 2010

103   http://www.economist.com/blogs/freeexchange/2011/02/energy_prices

be far worse than we now suspect, then all the government has to do is increase its carbon price accordingly. It does not have to start its whole planning process again from scratch.

Even better, a carbon tax doesn't depend on the right-eousness and self control of individuals – it works even if individuals are never aware it exists. A carbon tax requires no great change to the way our system of allocation works.

When trying to choose which of two cars to buy today, nobody expects you at the same time to decide the whole economic structure of the country. You don't have to decide which workers would be best employed where, or whether the country's scarce capital could be best used elsewhere. You don't have to make a statement about your moral views or virtue. You don't even need to know what taxes the car business has paid, and what for.

All you have to do is choose which car best fits your needs, and meets your own budget. That's it.

A carbon tax simply adds to a system that we already know works.

Green Technology

Surprisingly, economic development on its own can act as a catalyst making our technologies more environmentally friendly.

The richer we are, the more we seem to care about clear air and protecting our local woodland. In contrast, those living in developing nations such as those in sub-Saharan Africa have greater concerns than, say, the pollution that their factories are creating in their river systems.

Over the last few decades, airlines have worked hard to reduce the emissions produced by aeroplanes. The carbon monoxide emissions of transport in America are down 75 per cent in twenty-five years, while a car travelling at full speed now emits less pollution than a parked car in 1975 from leaks.[104]

---

104   Ridley, 2010, p. 17

But despite these encouraging changes, the severity of the situation means that we cannot rely on such effects to bring about a green world. Today, each extra pound of GDP activity requires less carbon than the last to be emitted into the atmosphere – a phenomenon experts term 'decoupling'– but the cumulative nature of growth means that nevertheless the total level of emissions continues to rise.

A carbon tax is not a magic wand. There are two ways to reduce the carbon output of today's economic activity. Either we develop technology that emits less, or alternatively we just have to undertake less economic activity in the first place.

If science and technology were to stand still, then a carbon tax by itself could not prevent a massive economic reorganisation, likely leading to a lower standard of living. This transition would of course be far more efficiently managed by a carbon tax than government plan, but we would be significantly poorer nevertheless. A carbon tax might not ban aviation, but it may mean you could only afford a few flights in your lifetime.

Now, a carbon tax does provide significant rewards to entrepreneurs and innovators looking to develop zero carbon technology. It makes sure there are real profits to be gained from the introduction of new technologies. If a company can develop zero carbon aviation, then it will face a significantly reduced tax bill, and accordingly be able to earn far greater profits.

But in a world without perfect markets, these incentives may in turn not be as perfect as we would like. It will make a large difference to future welfare whether the cost of adaptation is met more by new technology or by carbon austerity, and accordingly we would like to do as much as possible as a society to encourage the alternative provided by new technology.

In addition, even with the incentives provided by a new tax, it will take time for us to alter the way our society works. Our current institutions and technologies are so closely interconnected to old energy sources that in the short term our responsiveness to even large changes in price may be small. To completely wean us off carbon through higher prices alone will be extremely difficult, not least due to political difficulties.

Developing new green technologies is one of those cases where the existence of the 'positive externalities' is likely to have a significant impact. No entrepreneur will be able to capture all the benefit from a carbon-free plane, just as no entrepreneur could capture all the benefit from penicillin. Accordingly markets will allocate less investment to the field than might be optimal for society as a whole.

Furthermore, we are hardly starting from a vacuum. The UK's transport infrastructure doesn't exist unfettered in a prefect free market, but it is largely government controlled. It will have to be the government that alters its own infrastructure, or at least opens up access to new innovators and entrepreneurs. For example, there may be a role for government in supporting a national charging system for electric cars, or developing the electrification of the railways.

But such measures should be the exception rather than the rule. The record of targeted government subsidies for innovation is less promising than one might hope, and there is a reason that we generally do not trust the centre to 'pick winners'. Governments have been seeking alternative sources of energy for decades with limited success. The current system of UK subsidies for renewable energy seems designed perversely to subsidise most the least efficient methods of reducing carbon.[105] Bio fuels seem to have achieved little so far other than devastating rainforests, actually increasing carbon emissions, and sending food

---

105 Tim Worstall has a fuller explanation of this in his *Chasing Rainbows*, 2010, p. 92

prices soaring to such an extent that there were riots across the developing world in 2008.[106]

More to the point, it is no longer really true that the private sector is ignoring, if it ever did, the potential of green technology. Huge resources are being poured by venture capitalists into developing new carbon-free methods of energy, production and transportation. The private sector is very aware of the huge sums to be made, especially in a world where the price of fossil fuels continues to increase.

There is a case for limited subsidy for basic research, or speculative projects that may take decades to pay off. Indeed, there is a case for such support in most areas of science.

What we do not want or need are clumsy government attempts to pick the winning technology. The government will do best if it provides basic support – and then stands aside.

Defending Transport

We do not know how we will solve the problems climate change brings. There is no set path to take us from here to there. We do not know whether we will solve our fossil fuel addiction with more electric cars, greater public transport, some sort of geo-engineering – or perhaps a mix of all the three.

What we do know is that a green future will not be achieved by a government-led plan, a blizzard of new initiatives or new moral norms in society. Instead, our overwhelming priority should be the creation of an effective carbon tax, and alongside it limited subsidy for basic research and help implementing new ideas into government-controlled infrastructure.

More important than what these proposals imply is what they *don't* offer support for. We need to stop judging developments as 'green' and therefore 'good', rather than relying on 'fossil fuels' and therefore bad. If we've implemented the right carbon tax regime, then that question is simply wrong. The issue is not whether any particular development is good, but whether we can afford it.

In other words, that means no blanket opposition to the building of roads or limiting the expansion of airports. It means letting individuals rather than bureaucrats decide how we bring our level of carbon down.

Furthermore, it means accepting that we cannot reduce carbon everywhere at the same time. It is very difficult currently to create a carbon-free plane. As aviation is so important to the economy we may need to allow increased carbon emissions from the sector while we pursue greater cutbacks elsewhere. Many activists call such a situation unfair, but this is just silly. Making such decisions is what pragmatism is all about.

In fact, as long as the industry can afford its carbon bill, it really is none of the government's business whether a private company builds a new airport or not. If private individuals believe flying is worth the higher ticket prices that may come from a higher carbon tax, then private companies should be allowed to expand. If they don't, then the industry will naturally contract on its own.

The threat of climate change is a difficult issue which throws up numerous problems for our politics, economics, and international relationships. But we shouldn't let it be used as a front for other deep green or socialist agendas. The transport industry is not very different from any other sector of the economy, and it should be treated in the same way, expanding if it can afford a higher price for carbon, contracting if not. It is innovation that will ultimately slow or stop climate change, and that will only come from the private sector, not a government plan.

The environmental threat means we need less planning, not more.

INVESTMENT

It took Britain near thirty years to build a single new airport terminal.

The original debate over whether to build a fifth terminal for Heathrow began in 1982; a designer was chosen in 1989 and the formal proposal put forward in 1993. A public inquiry ran for four years from 1995–1999 and then on 20 November 2001 the project was finally given the go-ahead by the then transport minister, Stephen Byers. Construction began in 2002, and the new terminal finally opened in 2008, twenty-six years after debate initially began.

While booming Eastern economies add a vast network of new runways, High Speed Trains and motorways, Britain today largely has to get by with road and air networks designed in the 1950s, and a railway from Victorian times.

Unfortunately, Terminal Five is far from an isolated example.

A Crossrail railway line through central London has been dreamed of for nearly fifty years, and the current route finally identified in 1989. Unable to find parliamentary time in 1991 as interest fell because of the recession, the government finally abandoned the project in 1994. Ten years later in 2004 a new plan was submitted, and received parliamentary approval in 2008. Government agreed to finance the project in 2010. It is now expected to open in 2018.

Each time the project was delayed, huge costs were added. In 1980 the first Crossrail project was expected to cost £330m (£1.2bn in today's prices); the current project is projected at £16bn.[107] It is not only the government and

---

107   Rosewell, 2010

passengers that suffer from exploding costs, but owners of properties along the proposed route. Left in planning limbo, they suffer so-called 'blight' driving down the worth of their land. Nobody wants to buy a property if a railway might be constructed right next to or through it. Estimates suggest that around £8bn worth of land was left unused while waiting for government to come to its final decision.

Suppose you agree with this book's thesis that we need significant investments in transport. After years of debate, the current government is at last committed to the construction of a High Speed Rail network, making it its transport priority – nevertheless, the first stage of the railway from London to Birmingham is not expected to open till 2026, with an extension to Manchester and Leeds by 2033.[108] In roughly the same time, remember, the original railways expanded from 100 miles in 1830 to 6,600 miles in 1852.[109]

The reason why it takes us so long to build new infrastructure projects is not that British engineering companies are particular inefficient or slow. The delays starts long before the workers show up at the work site, in the original process of making a decision itself. The problem with UK infrastructure is not so much our builders as our planning process.

The current process for decisions has two stages: first, a detailed inquiry is held in which evidence and consultations are taken from experts and stakeholders. After the recommendations of this inquiry are made, the decision is then taken by the appropriate democratic body – normally Parliament itself, although local government can also have a say.

As we will see, neither of these two stages works well. The UK still relies on overly cautious, technocratic models to make its decisions and a short sighted political process.

---

108   High Speed Rail: Investing in Britain's Future Consultation, February 2011
109   Wolmar, Christian, *On the Wrong Line*, 2005, p. 5

Until we realise that we will never be able to plan perfectly the future, the UK will remain forever behind in its investment.

How Much is an Hour Worth?

If you examine the recent business case for the proposed High Speed 2 railway line carefully, you'll find that by far the biggest benefit predicted comes from something known as 'Time Savings', making up a colossal £17.9bn out of the £21.9bn predicted benefits.[110]

Of course, the decision on whether to proceed with any infrastructure project can be very complicated. Dozens of variables must be considered: will the project be commercially viable? Will it support local growth? What will be the knock-on traffic effects to other parts of the network? How many carbon emissions will its construction and use cause? How many people will lose their homes? How many will suffer from increased noise or air pollution?

Nevertheless, the chief factor that has controlled decisions over whether to proceed with transport investments in the last few years is not how many jobs they will save, but rather how much *time*. Unfortunately, as we will see, it is far from clear that this number actually has much scientific credibility behind it, or that it really catches what we find valuable about new investments.

The standard tool used in making such decisions is a process called cost-benefit analysis. In order to make the most reasoned decision, experts assemble models estimating the effects of new infrastructure on traffic, the economy and the environment. At the bottom line of these careful calculations is a Net Benefit Ratio (NBR), the ratio of benefits to costs.

While this process is supposed to be non partisan and strictly technocratic, long experience has taught government

110 Economic Case for HS2, February 2011

that the estimates produced by planners are often far too optimistic. As a measure of precaution, standard practice is only to proceed with a project if the ratio of benefits to costs is expected to be higher than two to one.

Part of the uncertainty comes because the government considers many other factors beyond strict commercial viability. A project that is predicted to make a direct loss may still be worth it if expected to boost wider economic growth. A highly profitable project may be rejected if it makes too negative an impact on the environment.

The main two benefits transport projects are normally expected to produce are the saving of passengers' time, and enhancements to the wider economy. The benefit from the time saved is normally predicted to be the larger of the two. A faster train line helps us get where need to go quicker, while a new road can ease congestion, and mean less time is wasted in traffic jams.

But how much exactly is this time worth?

By using a combination of experimental studies and looking carefully at current wage rates, economists believe they can make a reasonable estimate. Currently, the Department values a saved hour of leisure time at £4.46 per hour, and an hour of work at £26.73.[111] Over its lifetime, this can lead to significant assumed value from an asset: the Department calculated that the High Speed 2 railway line would save £28.7bn worth of time, while a theoretical third runway at Heathrow would have saved between £8.6 and £12.8bn.

This is clearly a crude measure at best. As opponents of the High Speed 2 train line have argued, it is probably too strong a point to claim that every hour a businessman spends on a train is entirely wasted. Both humans and the economy itself are not so efficient that we are fighting for every second we can get hold of.

111　　Rosewell, 2010

The only exact means of quantifying the worth of any hour saved is how much each of us would pay for it. But if this is the case, you may ask why government needs to subsidise these benefits at all. If a train that gets me home in half the time is worth an extra £20 to me, then a private company should be able to add this value to the cost of the ticket, and make its money back. The market will provide whatever new investment is worth the cost of construction. Why then does the government concern itself with fiddly, impossible-to-perfect projections of the value of time?

The answer is that the government doesn't believe pricing can perfectly capture all this value.

Assuming that the product meets your expectations, any good you buy in a market economy is by definition worth at least as much to you as you paid for it. If it weren't, you wouldn't have bought it. The difference between the absolute maximum you'd pay for any good and the amount you paid for it is known as the consumer surplus.

Companies would obviously love to be able to charge each customer a different price, set at the absolute most they'd be willing to be pay. In the real world this is impossible and this is generally a good thing for customers – except for those cases where the consumer surplus is the difference between whether an enterprise is profitable or otherwise. If I were willing to pay £20 for a new train journey but it doesn't go ahead as the maximum the company can charge is £10, then I am clearly worse off.

The notion of consumer surplus is mainstream economics, but of course, as an argument, this could apply to practically any good in the economy. There is always additional value for any good that companies cannot capture – that doesn't mean that in each case government should subsidise the market.

In short, being overly precise about the value of time saved by any new investment is probably misleading. Moreover, by fixating on it alone, we ignore other impacts which can be just as – if not more – important.

How Many Jobs Will a New Railway Line Bring?

If the value from time saved normally forms the biggest number in cost-benefit analysis, the question that matters most to politicians is: what will the impact of this development be on growth and jobs?

The studies normally consider these under the catch-all term of 'wider economic benefits'. For example, the Department for Transport has calculated £3.6bn of wider economic benefits from High Speed 2[112] and independent analysts suggested £20bn from a third runway at Heathrow.[113]

Several different effects are normally collected under this term. New developments allow more people to travel, improving capacity.[114] Then there are 'agglomeration effects'. As we have seen, when people live closely together in big cities they tend to be more productive. New transport developments allow more people to live closely together, and in this way can drive further growth. The more people who can work in London, the faster our economy will growth.

If there is one lesson from the history of transport, it is the importance that the sector can have on the wider economy. New forms of transport can fundamentally alter the way our cities and industries work. There would be no Liverpool or New York without their ports, and no Industrial Revolution without the steam train.

---

112 High Speed Rail London to the West Midlands and Beyond, High Speed 2 Ltd, 2010, p. 176

113 Economic Impact of Hub Airports, British Chambers of Commerce, 2009, pp. 6,7

114 Under certain assumptions, strictly speaking this effect should be captured in the value attributed to the value of time saved. Recognising that this is unlikely to be the case in the real world, official estimates make an additional 10 per cent allowance on top of that figure for 'imperfect competition'. This figure seems to be somewhat arbitrary.

However, it does not follow that we can predict or even measure the impact any particular project will have on the wider economy. There are some things that just can't be planned, and the future path of the economy is one of them.

Too often the plans are written as if the economy is already practically perfectly efficient, needing only minor tweaks to carry it forward. If your economic model assumes that whatever happens Britain will always see trend growth in the future of 2 per cent a year, then clearly it is pointless to spend lots of money on investment for growth that will happen anyway.

Ironically, the Planners are showing far more blind faith in free markets and perfect competition than any neoliberal economist. The truth is that our economy isn't perfect. There are always ways of improving it, although no central plan can tell us what they are. Trying to fiddle around with market prices and structures to maximise sometimes nebulous concepts of 'consumer surplus' is an exercise in futility. By trying to improve one part of the economy, we may end up damaging another.

Just as entrepreneurs can never fully know whether an enterprise will succeed, leaders sometimes simply have to make an educated guess. No economic projection favoured the building of Canary Wharf, and there were severe doubts about the need for the extension to the Jubilee Line. Both have been huge successes.

While numbers are important, they are not the whole story. Other effects can be harder to quantify, but that doesn't mean we should ignore them. There is always the danger of falling into the trap of the proverbial drunk who searches for his keys under a streetlight, simply because that is where the light is.

That is not to say that there is no value from writing a business plan, or the process of running a cost-benefit analysis. The best business plans aren't designed to be a perfect map for the business's future. Instead, they are tools to organise the entrepreneur's thinking, to think through what assumptions he is making, check his numbers make sense and run scenario plans. We should try to think of cost-benefit analysis in the same way: a technique to show what assumptions we are making and what still remains unknown.

As writer Tim Harford has argued,

> politicians have [too often] demanded the appearance of certainty where certainty cannot exist... a spuriously precise number becomes the focus for all debate... There are many ways for a conclusion to look statistically robust but be wrong. What is needed is to be clear about the underpinning assumptions and open-minded about what would happen if the assumptions were mistaken.[115]

NBRs and economic benefits are too often given the status of absolute truth in the wider political debate, but can never be more than educated guesses. Both the economy and traffic itself are chaotic in structure and impossible to predict in anything other than the broadest brushstrokes. Yet these numbers are often the most concrete factors in the analysis – other variables such as the value of time saved, the costs of environmental or historical damage, or the effects on inequality are hopelessly relativistic.

We need then to be more impressionistic in our own judgements as well. A proposed project we estimate will cause *so* much economic activity and save *so* much time, but, on the other hand, will cause *this* much damage to the environment and *this* much upheaval to locals. Having a feel for the magnitudes of each of these variables is useful; trying to merge them all into a single number is likely to create confusion rather than clarity.

---

115 http://timharford.com/2011/04/why-wepercentE2percent80per cent99re-all-far-too-sure-of-ourselves/

The Problems with Politics

Sometimes, frustrated technocrats look enviously at the more authoritarian countries of East Asia. Democracy is all well and good, but single-party countries have it far easier implementing controversial pieces of infrastructure: from Singapore's 1975 introduction of the world's first congestion charge to China's rapid construction of new motorway and high speed rail networks. It is much easier to implement sweeping change when one doesn't have to worry about appeasing special interests or displaced local residents.

The planning system often tests the weaknesses in our democracy. Decisions are inevitably controversial. Nobody wants a new motorway built in their backyard, or for their home to be compulsorily purchased. There are few worse pictures in the media than bulldozers tearing up a nature reserve or a wrecking ball taking out a church. While criticism and protest will be immediate and visceral, any benefits are likely to be enjoyed only many years from now when the politician who made the decision is long out of office. Voters are not known for being grateful for political bravery shown decades in the past.

Indeed, democracy is hardly a perfect system. It has flaws: politicians are only human, and respond only too well to electoral incentives. It is noticeable that the decision on the Humber Bridge bypass in 1966 was taken at the same time as Barbara Castle was facing a difficult by-election; or more recently, that the go ahead to Crossrail was given in the run up to Gordon Brown's 2007 election that never was.

It is likely that to some extent the political class themselves, cut off in a metropolitan bubble, are too easily swayed by lobbyists and groupthink rather than the views of the nation.

Ultimately however, politicians depend on the voters for their position, and sometimes the voters themselves can be even more timid than the politicians. Voters often seem risk averse, overly nostalgic about the past and scared of change, inconsistent in their preferences, and confused about basic economics.[116]

The situation can be worse at the local level, where voters are understandably adamant that they don't want new infrastructure built in their backyard. The negative effects of investment tend to be far more concentrated than the dispersed gains. Far more people gain from a new train line than have to suffer from the new line spoiling their view. It is the latter group who will, however, be far more motivated to make a stand at the ballot box.

At the same time, national decision-making is hardly free from its own political distortions. Politicians are instinctively attracted to 'grand projects' that leave them a clear physical legacy, and tend to be too optimistic about both costs and benefits. We might call it Millenium Dome syndrome.

Worse than this, centralised institutions cannot have the information and authority to micromanage local facilities. From the lofty height of the national level, it is hard to introduce serious political accountability for the fine details of any particular local transport project.

Frustrated by these difficulties, in its final years New Labour tried to take out the politics from planning. Rather than leave crucial national decisions to the whims of the electorate, it created a new body, the Independent Planning Commission (IPC). The IPC was an independent commission of experts, acting as neutral adjudicators on planning decisions, and basing their decisions on a series of National Policy Statements created by government. Crucially, it was to work with a nine-month deadline from application to decision.

But just as there is no perfect model that can ennumerate the full benefits and costs from any project, there is no real

---

116   For a good summary see Bryan Caplan, *The Myth of the Rational Voter*

way to take out the politics from planning. Infrastructure projects often require the use of Compulsory Purchase Orders, the needs of the nation overriding the property rights of the few. Decisions are often unavoidably political, the interests of different groups clashing against each other. They will be much easier to swallow if voters feel some ownership in the decision, rather than having it imposed on them.

Ultimately, trying to remove the politics from the decision proved impossible. No matter how impressive in its credentials any new panel is, government will always eventually find itself having to express an opinion. No government could have completely washed its hands of the decision of whether to build a third runway or not.

Whether we like it or not, the UK is not China. Giving the Planners absolute power is not the answer. While that means that it may take longer to gain voter approval for any particular project, the benefits of democracy far outweigh its costs. The way to improve the way the UK makes planning decisions is to correct the often perverse political incentives that currently operate, rather than try to sidestep democracy altogether.

For a start, we can at least try to make larger decisions quicker, and in situations which require no subsidy we can move more to assumptions in favour of development. Governments and councils should have to prove the harmful effects of new developments, not developers prove that they are needed.

Some decisions relate to national priorities, and therefore should be made by national bodies such as Parliament. It is the country as a whole that should make choices over whether a high speed rail network or new runway should be built, and then in turn committees can decide exact routes and compensation for locals.

But for other decisions, we should over time aim for a significant devolution of political power away from the centre. It should be local communities that decide for themselves whether they are really getting value from the subsidy of local transport networks, or whether the money could be best invested elsewhere. Concerns over the harm to the local environment are likely to diminish when the benefits are also visible locally.

There is a downside to giving local communities greater control. If the problem with trade unions is that they often ignore the interests of workers outside the company, the problem with local communities is that they ignore the interests of those who don't yet live in the community. A new road may allow thousands more homes to be built, but this will matter little to you if all it does is spoil your view.

At the same time local councils have little incentive to fund new developments either. Much of the increased revenue that any new development brings in will simply be collected back by the central state.

We need to give both current residents and their councils share in the benefits of new developments. Part of the answer may be a parallel devolution of financing with political power, allowing councils to keep more of the revenues which businesses in their areas produce.

One method that has been moderately successful in the US is the practice of 'tax increment financing'. Under such schemes, local authorities can fund new developments by borrowing the capital against the increase in tax revenues they expect to receive. London Mayor Boris Johnson is currently looking to extend the southern end of the Northern line of the London Underground out to Battersea through just a scheme.

Ultimately no set of measures will give us perfect predictions about the costs and benefits of any project, or allow us to make instant, fair decisions. Nevertheless, we remain still in the Churchillian position of 'democracy [being] the worst form of government except all the others that have been tried'. More planning is not the answer.

Should We Build High Speed Rail?

In 2011, the country is currently in the midst of a years-long debate over the costs and merits of creating a new High Speed Rail network.

Furious debate centres on increasingly technical questions. How many passengers do we think will take the railway in twenty years' time, and how reliable do we think these estimates to be? How many people will shift their journey from the air, and take the new train instead? How many new jobs will the new line create? To what extent is time spent on a train wasted?

These are good questions to ask, but we shouldn't pretend we'll ever have perfect answers. We will never know for sure whether we are making the right decision, no matter how long we agonise over cost-benefit studies. In the best scenario, the new lines will see a renaissance in our northern cities, fundamentally altering the economic geography of the UK. In the worst, passenger numbers barely rise and it turns out to have been an expensive distraction from more pressing problems.

In any case, the argument for the new line doesn't depend on trading back and forth ever more finely calibrated economic studies. Instead, we have to be far more strategic and holistic, looking at the case for the new network in the whole. While there is always a possibility that any new investment will be a failure, as an already compact country the UK is likely to benefit disproportionately from a new network compared to other countries. Fast, efficient links can help the rest of the country share London's success.

Over the last few decades, we have extended our planning processes in an effort to make our estimates more accurate and our judgements more inclusive. Whether this has worked is debatable. What is sure is that the process of doing so has made it harder to get new investment projects off the ground and, in the long run, hurt us all.

Limiting the time that an inquiry can take to make a

decision, or creating an assumption in favour of development, can seem like crude measures. However, if we accept that we can never make perfect decisions, then perhaps at least we ought to try to make them faster.

REGULATION

Despite the worldwide privatisation movement of the last thirty years, the initial worries that led governments to take transport under its own control have not gone away. Transport is too important to the economy, it is still thought, to relinquish control entirely. Transport is just too riddled with effects and externalities that couldn't perfectly be captured by the market.

Instead, the reformers of the last thirty years sought to create new institutions that would combine the best aspects of public and private sectors. Governments believed that with the right regulations they could make new industries that would not only be efficient and innovative, but fair and affordable as well. Governments wanted to be sure that they had enough control to ensure that ticket prices could not soar too high, or that companies didn't stop serving isolated rural communities that could never be directly profitable.

But throughout transport's history, regulation has always caused as many problems as it solves.

By mandating maximum prices too low for companies to make a profit in the early twentieth century, governments helped kill off the original American and British private railway companies. Today, price regulation makes already busy airports such as Heathrow more crowded. Regulators have been unable to keep costs down in private companies, and the cost reductions they have achieved have sometimes led to railway and airports prioritising retail revenue over passenger comfort. As we'll see in Chapter 7, the record of safety regulation is little better.

Worst of all, by removing companies' discretion and autonomy, regulation has made it harder for companies to innovate and take risks. Regulation captures companies, fossilising them at a particular point in time, not letting them develop as the world changes.

Our over reliance on regulation is holding back the innovation in transport we so desperately need.

A Parable of Rail

To see why, suppose for a moment that you were the CEO and founder of a small railway company operating in an isolated rural county. Your railway gently meanders from the nearest big city through several sleepy towns, and although the scenery is beautiful, the rolling landscape keeps costs high. The service acts as a lifeline to many of these otherwise isolated communities, but unfortunately the small size means that passenger numbers are low. It is difficult if not impossible for you to break even.

Nevertheless, the government recognises your value to the community – and the political backlash that would occur if the service was withdrawn. You and the government do a deal. The government will subsidise your service by £50 million a year, just enough to make sure that, on your Financial Director's latest projections, you break even.

But then, alas, disaster strikes. The economy hits a recession, and your already meagre passenger numbers fall further. Reluctantly you head to the nearest proverbial government office, and inform them sadly that without a further £10 million in subsidy you will have to go out of business.

Very, very reluctantly the man in the government passes on the money, and disaster is averted for another day. However, he does make sure to put in place a few conditions. Since the government is passing on so much money, it's only fair that it has a bit more say about what the money is used for. Perhaps you could put on a few more trains and keep the waiting rooms open later? And then, since the government is sharing in the bad times, it only seems fair that it enjoys the proceeds when good times come again.

Almost as reluctantly you agree to these conditions, and go back to your newly secure company.

Fortunately, the economy does turn itself around again, to such an extent that soon your enthusiastic Chief Operating Officer is coming to your office with all sorts of exciting new ideas for services and ways to raise funds.

But, while the ideas do indeed sound exciting, you can't help but hesitate. The 'few small suggestions' from the government had turned out to be a long list of new requirements and specifications. You're not sure how these new ideas will fit in with the rules already set down, and you don't quite fancy the hassle of having to restart the negotiations all over again.

And, of course, the problem with exciting new ideas is that they have a tendency to go wrong. They introduce risk, and risk only seems worthwhile if there's some upside at the end of it. After all, even if these new plans make millions in new profits, the man in government will only demand his share of the money. You've already put down in writing what your predicted profits are – best to stick to that plan.

In any case, that plan is safe. What harm is there in coasting along, and running matters in the same way as you've always done? Whatever happens, the nice man in the government will make sure that you don't lose too much money.

No, all things considered, best to shut up the excitable Chief Operating Officer. New ideas can wait for some other day.

The Problem of Risk

This situation, more or less, is both the problem the government often faces whenever it tries to control prices or use subsidy, and the way in which railway franchise contracts worked.

Risk is fundamental to business. In a world where the future can't always be planned, risk exists in any significant decision. Perhaps a new innovation will fail, the market will turn or cultural tastes change. It is impossible to know.

Often, the government is tempted to take responsibility for risk itself. As the government has much lower borrowing costs, it is often cheaper for it to keep control rather than try and pass it onto the private sector. A millionaire will require a much lower potential of reward than the average man to bet a thousand pounds.

Even more than this, the government often can't pass on risk and control even if it wanted to. Both it and the private sector know very well that electoral realities mean that it is never going to let a railway just shut down or entirely go bust.

Trying to compensate companies for bad luck is far from straightforward. Sometimes things go wrong because of circumstances far beyond our control. Other times they go wrong because of our own mistakes.

But if we can't tell the difference between the two we risk bailing companies out for their own bad business decisions, or, conversely, harshly penalising them for matters outside their own control. Just as bad, if we perfectly smooth out their income, there are no incentives for the private sector to take risks or innovate. What's the point of taking chances if the government will make up your revenue anyway?

The way governments try to avoid this trap is through independent regulators who can determine what costs are a company's own fault, and which are the result of poor market conditions. Unfortunately, this is still inevitably a judgement call, with no perfect answer.

Regulators are often accused of being 'captured' by their industries. In practice they find that they have to rely on the companies they regulate for their information on the state of the industry. Inevitably the industry's worldview to some effect affects them, and they start to share its assumptions.

A key problem is that it's simply impossible for external overseers to know which costs are really necessary, and which could be cut down by more innovative management. In a free market, the competition of other firms ensures that all costs have to be kept down, but in monopolies or industries reliant on government subsidy, this market discipline simply doesn't exist.

Without perfect information, regulators cannot make perfect decisions. Whenever government tries to control the profits or prices of an industry, they inevitably end up blunting incentives, reducing innovation and unfairly bailing companies out.

In the privatised railways, this has resulted in a phenomenon known as cap-and-collar contracts. In order to try and shield private companies from the risks from economic downturn, the government guarantees a railway franchise its revenue. If revenue falls below 95 per cent of the forecast revenue, the government promises to make up the difference. However, the flip side is that if revenue is more than 5 per cent above the company's initial projections, the government will confiscate the surplus.

The advantage of this system is that government doesn't have to promise enormous profits up front to tempt private sector investors to invest their money. The downside is that it reduces the incentives to the train franchise to try and improve its position – what is the point when the government will take the extra revenues and make up for losses anyway?

The Wise Investor
Let us return to our small countryside railway line.

Exciting news comes through that the government has announced the construction of a new town near your line. If you could persuade enough investors, for the small price of a billion pounds you could construct a new extension to the town and make large profits.

Excited by your new plan, you set off to the big city, business plan in hand. Your Chief Financial Officer has looked through the numbers carefully, and concluded that the project makes financial sense as long as you can charge around £10 a ticket – around £5 for the running costs, and £5 to pay back the investors who gave the initial capital.

But to your horror, none of the cynical city investors will back your scheme.

Why?

They don't trust the government.

'The problem,' one wise investor explains, 'is that the government has you where it wants you.'

'Suppose I were to give you my money now, and you went on to build this new railway. What would happen next?'

Confused, you point again to your carefully put together business plan, and the revenue that your £10 tickets will rake in.

'Ah,' but the investor goes on. 'Perhaps you will charge £10 in year one. But what about year two? I'm afraid, the government will say, that we have a clear example of abuse of monopoly here, charging more for a service than it costs you to run. £5 a ticket would seem more appropriate.'

Dumbfounded, you try to explain that on £5 a ticket you would never make your money back, but the investor interrupts you again, 'Indeed. But the railway's already built. What would you do with it?'

And you realise that in such a situation your best choice would be to keep the service running after all. You'd still lose a lot of money, but perhaps you'd minimise your losses.

'You see,' the investor finishes. 'the government gets a brand new railway line, and it doesn't have to pay for the privilege. As I said – it has you where it wants you.'

Giving up, you sadly throw your new business plan into the nearest bin.

On Terrorism and Odysseus

The problem with transport investment is that its new infrastructure takes the form of sunk costs.

It takes up a lot of capital to build up a Google or a McKinsey as well, but if the government treats such companies badly they can always move to countries that will welcome their contribution.

Transport companies by contrast have to suffer the regulations of whatever country they are located in. As transport industries are prone to create local monopolies, governments have all the excuse they need to interfere with prices if they want to. But if investors don't believe the government will allow them to earn the full profits from their investments, then they are unlikely to want to invest very much in the first place.

This, of course, is bad for everyone. The investors don't get to make the profits they could have, and the country doesn't get the new infrastructure it badly needs. The government can try and make initial promises to allow profits in future years but talk, after all, is cheap.

This is what is known as time inconsistency – or more popularly, the 'We do not negotiate with terrorists' principle. As a general rule of thumb, governments are very aware that every time they negotiate with terrorists or tax away profits, they are only encouraging more terrorists and less investment. But every time they find themselves with a gun to their head or a chance for some pre-election giveaways, they simply can't help themselves.

The general solution to such conundrums is to deliberately restrict your options. The example to follow is that of Odysseus, tying himself to the mast of his ship to ensure he could avoid any temptation from the lure of the beautiful Sirens' song.

In particular, governments make use of several policy options that in law tie their hands, making sure that they can't touch future profits and that the original investors get paid back.

The simplest solution is something called rate-of-return regulation. Under this system, the government allows all costs and a small profit margin to be passed directly through to the prices charged to customers, guaranteeing companies that they will make their money back.

But this is not how investment works in the real world. Sometimes companies open new railway lines, their demand forecasts turn out to be spectacularly wrong, and they go bust.

Worse, although we have removed the government's ability to exploit railway companies, we have made it possible for railway companies to exploit customers instead.

Normally a company has to keep tight control on costs. Extra costs are only worthwhile if they mean extra profits.

But in this situation the company is guaranteed to get its costs back, and a small profit margin on top. The more costs the better. It is time to order in the most luxurious of trains, each seat with a dedicated flat screen TV and drink holder. No need to shop around too hard for the cheapest supplier either.

When this rate-of-return system was tried in the US for in the mid twentieth century, it was soon discovered that it led to grossly inflated prices.[117] Although the regulators did try to put some controls on costs, putting it through a 'used-and-useful' test, in practice it found it impossible to judge what was necessary investment and what over indulgence. Costs to consumers increased, and efficiency sank.

Determined to avoid such cost increases, when it came to refine the market structures for the newly privatised UK railways, the government was committed to avoiding this fate. It devised a new policy invention, the so-called Regulatory Asset Base that it believed could avoid past mistakes.

But has it worked?

---

117   Helm, Dieter, 'Utility regulation, the RAB and the cost of capital', Oxford, 2009

The Return to Nationalisation?

The Regulatory Asset Base is an unfortunately complicated sounding phrase for an unfortunately complicated policy tool. Nevertheless, the questions around how it works, its strengths and weaknesses are at the heart of many of the dilemmas our transport system currently faces. RABs (for short) are at the heart of how Network Rail and our airports plan their funding, and how regulators decide what prices to charge. They offer the potential for unlocking important new private funding in our roads or energy systems. If Britain needs a significant leap in the amount it invests in infrastructure, then many experts believe that RABs are a significant part of the answer.

Here was the plan: the Regulatory Asset Base would avoid the twin pitfalls of government total control or nationalisation, and allowing private companies more freedom, but seeing costs soar at the same time.

Most basically, the RAB is just a number. This number represents the amount of capital invested in a business. When a private sector company such as Tesco invests £1bn of their own capital, they might hope to receive a 10 per cent annual return, or £100m a year. Similarly, if a train company has invested £1bn then it hopes the regulator will allow a similar £100m in returns. This profit pays back the investors who have lent the initial capital, either as a direct loan or in equity as shares.

The clever part of the RAB is that it allows private companies to enjoy the same cheap costs of borrowing as the government. The return on the RAB is guaranteed by the regulator (and ultimately the state), meaning that lending towards an RAB is practically the same as lending to a government.

But what should the level of RAB be? For one thing, many transport companies own significant capital inherited from the government – how should this be valued? At what level should be it depreciated? How much is any train line, say, really worth?

Fundamentally these are unanswerable questions, and so in practice the regulators have been forced to work backwards. They set the level of the RAB so that it produces what they believe to be a suitable rate of return. Unfortunately, this brings us back to the problems of inflated costs, and trying to avoid paying companies for investment that later turns out to be useless.

It also raises another difficulty. What should this rate of return be?

In a market system, we normally think of return as related to risk. The riskier the asset, the more profit an investor will need to make it worthwhile. When raising capital, companies have to make their own decision between how much money to make through loans, and how much through issuing shares. No entrepreneur wants to face massive loan payments if the business doesn't go to plan, but then neither does he want to sell away a share of his company and any profits. Each business has to make its own decision, choosing how to structure its debts depending on the risks inherent in the enterprise.

One of the problems with the RAB concept is that it is not clear exactly what risks *are* inherent in the business. The regulator normally assigns a rate of return that assumes a mixture of debt and equity, but as economist Dieter Helm has pointed out, this only makes sense if the private companies really are facing risk. For a risk free return, it is always cheaper to take out a loan.

This is more or less what we see private sector companies doing. Institutions are gearing up with enormous levels of debt, precisely because they believe there is no risk that they won't be paid back.

This is a neat piece of financial arbitrage, allowing companies to make profits without taking any risks. The company is paid more for taking on the more expensive form of equity debt, buys lower cost debt and then reaps the difference.

It is for precisely this reason that we have seen the amount of debt Network Rail holds continually increasing. The financial incentives that the government has put in place are all pushing it towards taking out bigger loans, safe in the knowledge that the taxpayer will be there to make the necessary payments in the future.

Besides the costs to ordinary customers, there are several problems with this. Firstly, it makes the company less flexible in future, locking in high levels of interest payment that will have to be paid for years. Moreover, by pushing out equity share ownership, it reduces private sector oversight over the company, burdening the regulator with more responsibility.

RABs have their uses, but they are not a sure means for unlocking risk free investment. Most fundamentally, if the government is in control of what counts for the RAB, then the government is in charge of what capital should be invested where. Government makes the plans, private investors provide the capital and customers pay the bills. It might not be called nationalisation, but the effects seem largely the same.

Why do Airports Contain so Many Shops?

No transport industry has suffered as much from regulation as the aviation industry. Ever since its creation, byzantine international treaties have dictated exactly which airlines can fly where. For much of its history, the industry's prices were determined by a deliberate cartel, the International Air Transport Association (IATA), while government subsidy kept national flag carriers viable.

In the last thirty years reformers have sought to liberalise the industry, opening up markets and driving down prices. The result has been a new era of budget airlines, and flying has become more affordable than ever before. At the same time, much of this excess regulation still exists , and is as much a cause of frequent complaints as any flaws deriving from the private sector.

Take the number of shops you find in our major airports. Sometimes they seem more like shopping malls than transport terminals. Heathrow alone contains 48,000 square metres of retail space, making it second only to Dubai for duty-free shops. The new Terminal Five apparently chooses to concentrate on promoting British brands such as Mulberry, Paul Smith and Smythson, while in Terminal Three you can find designer clothes from Armani, Gucci, or Cartier.[118]

These shops and the rent they pay are a large source of revenue for the airports. In many cases, over half of the revenue from the average passenger can originate from the shops they visit rather than the aeroplanes they actually board.

As in the railway market, prices for our leading airports are set by a regulator, in this case the Civil Aviation Authority (CAA). As retail is such a strong source of profit for airports, the CAA takes this revenue into account when deciding its pricing limits. In some cases, this can result in the maximum price for an airplane slot being set at below the actual cost of providing it. The regulator simply assumes that the airport will make the difference through its profits from shopping. This is known as the 'single till' system.

The problem is that these limits force airports to dedicate their resources towards increasing the space for shops, rather than increasing the comfort of passengers. When you are dependent on the revenue from retail just to break even, it is no surprise that more shops take a higher priority than more benches for customers.

---

118   http://news.cheapflights.co.uk/2011/04/top-ten-airports-for-shopping/

Aside from their retail businesses, airports are in the business of selling flight slots to airlines. At popular airports such as Heathrow, there are never enough slots to go around, and so these slots have to be rationed. Following international regulation this is largely done on a 'grand-fathering' basis. Airlines which hold slots in one season are allowed to maintain them in the next, as long as they can run a service on at least 80 per cent of their allocated slots. In addition there exists a secondary market in which airlines are allowed to sell their spare slots, although this does not seem to have seen a significant amount of activity.

Despite the shortage of capacity, since Heathrow's prices were first regulated in 1987 its prices have dropped from some of world's highest to being relatively low.

In other words, we have a good of which there is limited supply and ever increasing demand. The normal market way to deal with this is for prices to rise. Instead, we are deliberately holding prices down.

This is strange enough in itself. It becomes ever stranger when you consider our general aviation policy. This book may disagree with it, but after all the thrust of government policy is to reduce the amount of people flying, or at least limit its growth. It is bizarre that, while strictly limiting capacity, government is simultaneously holding the price down.

What would happen, if instead, we started again?

Let's look at first principles. Aviation slots are a commodity with excess demand and limited supply. The best way to ration such a commodity is through a price system. Just as the best way to ration limited road space is through prices, the best way to ration limited airport space is by putting a monetary value on it.

The easiest way to do this is to auction off each slot. This would mean that each slot would go to the airline who can use it best. Rather than rely on bureaucracy and precedent, we could let the market match up slots and airlines more efficiently.

In order to make this work, we would first have to abolish all limits on prices, allowing them to find their natural market level.

This has multiple advantages. Airlines can once again focus on maximising their service to passengers, rather than becoming ever larger shopping centres. It raises new funds which can be used for more investment in facilities.

Even better, it creates more effective competition between Heathrow and the other airlines. Imagine if Ferrari could only charge the same rates for its cars as a Mini. What would soon happy is that every Ferrari would rapidly sell out, and we'd see a long waiting list. Customers would enthusiastically clamour for increases in Ferrari production, and be uninterested in the possibilities of any new car manufacturer.

In the same way, if it does turn out that airlines can earn more per passenger at Heathrow than Gatwick, then they should have to pay more to operate at Heathrow. Alternatively, other airlines might discover that Heathrow isn't quite as valuable as they first thought, and instead make a profit by operating from Gatwick or Stansted.

Despite these advantages, there will still be many objections to such a reform. Let's run through them quickly.

To start with, there is already considerable controversy over who actually owns the property rights in airline slots. Many airlines have made significant investments on the basis of their own presumed ownership. It is unreasonable to redistribute the slots or for prices to jump in one year. Yet it is reasonable for prices to increase gradually over a longer period, of say ten years. Similarly, by randomly choosing a tenth of the slots to auction each year we could gradually free up the market, while still allowing the airlines ample time to recoup their investment.

Then there are the problems of monopoly. What if the airlines are right, and, thanks to its status as a hub airport, Heathrow really is a monopoly?

This is a real danger, but even if we remove the pricing limits we already have other protections for customers. If Heathrow really does have a damaging monopoly, the Competition Commission can intervene, as they already have done repeatedly to break BAA apart.

There is, however, no need to assume monopoly abuse, or that Gatwick won't be able to compete with Heathrow. Indeed, the assumption that Gatwick couldn't properly compete with Heathrow would be a lot easier to accept if the regulator had not spent the last twenty years holding Heathrow's prices down at a level where the second airport would always struggle.

Another objection will be that if Heathrow is allowed to raise its prices to airlines, then this may feed through to a rise in ticket prices to consumers. On the other hand this need not be a huge price increase – airport charges only account for about 4 per cent of airlines operating costs.[119] Any effects they might have are likely to be dwarfed by other government tax changes, such as the rise in Air Passenger Duty.

It is probably right that the price of flying from Heathrow goes up. Consumers have to be prepared to pay the full costs of their chosen activities. If they wish to fly at a crowded, popular airport then they should have to pay more for it. We cannot continue a policy of attempting to hold ticket prices down while complaining about increases in demand.

A final objection is that the extra revenue will end up as excess profit for BAA. This is true, but then, in the long run, excess profit is often an important part of a market system. It signals the presence of excess demand, and the need for new entrants and capacity. The best long-term way to cut prices of a good is to increase supply.

---

119 Papatheodorou, Andreas, Corporate rivalry and market power: competition issues in the tourism industry, p. 79

While the excess number of shops and crowded nature of Heathrow are frequent grievances, they are of course far from the most common complaints. To look at those, we will have to turn instead and look at the effects, positive and otherwise, of our ever increasing amount of safety regulation.

SAFETY

If you've taken a trip by air in the last ten years, you have some experience of what it now takes to board a plane.

Arriving at the airport, passengers are forced to comply with an increasingly authoritarian range of searches. In the last few years alone, we've seen new rituals such as the removal of shoes, the banning of drinking water on planes, and mandatory naked X-ray scans (or gropes) of every passenger. Sometimes, this descends into farce, as in the industry's confusion over whether an iPad should count as a laptop or not.

But is this really making us safer, or is it just another example of so-called 'safety theatre'?

Security today is still far from foolproof. In December 2009, for example, a businessman in Texas boarded a plane with a loaded handgun in his laptop case. He had forgotten to take it out, and security simply missed it on their screen. The US government regularly tests its security systems by sending its own agents through security with concealed weapons. Scarily, estimates suggest that as many as 70 per cent of these weapons are missed.[120]

The vulnerabilities of human nature are as important as any sophisticated security equipment. Tired security guards facing a monotonous series of X-rays can't be blamed if occasionally they do miss things. While the guard may be used to seeing scissors or oversized bottles of liquid

---

120 http://www.whatmakesthemclick.net/2011/02/10/100-things-you-should-know-about-people-58-people-see-what-they-expect-to-see/

in luggage a dozen times a day, their mind is simply not primed for noticing a weapon.

Once on the plane, the security measures continue.

No matter how many times passengers have flown in a plane, a polite fiction exists that they will stop for five minutes to watch a security demonstration. Statistically the chances that any of this will help anybody are tiny – but the losses in human time are enormous.

While safety regulations can and do save lives, as with everything, there are diminishing returns and costs to be paid. As we will see, it is far from clear that all the measures we have implemented in the roads, rail and air are worth the price. As much as you try to plan safety, it's impossible to completely take out the human factor.

Myths and Theatre

Throughout history, there have been transport incidents so severe that they've burned themselves into our consciousness: the RMS *Titanic* sinking into the cold north Atlantic waters in 1912; the 1937 inferno of the *Hindenberg* zeppelin, or the 1952 implosion of a test aeroplane at the Farnborough air show.

Safety brings up painful emotions, and it is not surprising that in the wake of such tragedies we turn to moral outrage. No human life is worth saving a few extra pennies. We remember that hundreds died on the *Titanic* because the White Star Line did not carry enough lifeboats. Never again can we risk that private greed or weakness stand in the way of appropriate safety procedures.

This moral feeling is absolute in its tone: to think of compromising between human life and cost is inhuman. Whenever an incident occurs, we are unwilling to listen to excuses or claims that it was 'just an accident'. We follow our innate human tendency to look for someone to blame, and usually we find that villain in the transport companies themselves.

Safety is clearly important. But for all our outrage and passion, we can often be far from rational when it comes to how to save lives.

Sometimes the facts are simply counterintuitive. In their *Freakonomics* books, Steven Levitt and Steven Dubner have near made a career of unravelling the myths behind transport safety. Car safety seats don't necessarily make you any safer. It can be just as, or more, dangerous to walk home drunk as to drive drunk (they recommend taking a taxi).

Statistically, some of the risk factors that do seem to make a difference in terms of safety include your gender, your age, the length of time you've driven, the time of day you're driving, your focus on the road, your profession, your marital status, your personality, your speed and, of course, your sobriety.[121] Some of these we can alter, others seem harder to change.

The most obvious place to spot our irrationality is in our relative reaction to the different safety records of various methods of transport. Most of us feel safest when driving our own cars, are not particularly worried about trains, but inwardly quake every time a plane hits turbulence – this despite the fact that the safety risks of aviation and driving are largely equivalent.[122]

The impact of human psychology is powerful. We have an innate tendency to be terrified of great heights. Plane accidents are far more likely to be reported in the media. They make better pictures, and after all car accidents are far too common to be newsworthy.

Governments don't just feel a responsibility to make us safer, but to make us *feel* safer. It is for this reason that

---

121 Vanderbilt, 2008, Chapter 9
122 The exact comparison depends on the type of driving. Not surprisingly, driving drunk at 3 a.m. on a Saturday night is far more dangerous than flying, while driving twelve hours later and sober on a clear motorway may be very marginally safer.

they are often tempted to indulge in examples of security theatre, in particular in the aviation sector. In the months after the terrorist attacks of September 11, for example, the National Guard posted armed soldiers at US airports – but these guards' guns contained no bullets.[123]

American security expert Bruce Schneier is a fierce critic of the recent aviation security measures, arguing that only two changes have made a significant difference to safety in the last ten years: reinforced cabin doors and the increased alertness of fellow passengers. Confiscating liquids, making passengers take off shoes and the new naked scanning machines, he argues, are largely a waste of time. Every time we introduce new security measures to tackle the last threat, we simply make the terrorists minutely adjust their plans. As Schneier argues, 'We screen for guns and bombs, so the terrorists use box cutters. We confiscate box cutters and corkscrews, so they put explosives in their sneakers. We screen footwear, so they try to use liquids. We confiscate liquids, so they put PETN bombs in their underwear.'[124]

PETN, or pentaerythritol tetranitrate in full, is the new favoured explosive of groups such as al Qaeda and thus the nightmare of security services. Unfortunately, it is both relatively compact and unable to be detected by sniffer dogs or traditional scanners. It is next to impossible to stop it completely or detect it without the kind of extremely invasive searches we currently reserve for expected drug smugglers. Ultimately, our best chance of stopping future terror attacks is probably through better intelligence, not ever more advanced scanning systems.

The Human Problem
If humans can be irrationally scared of generally safe forms of transport such as aviation, they can be just as irrationally

---

123   http://www.schneier.com/essay-299.html
124   http://www.schneier.com/essay-330.html

overconfident of their own abilities when they themselves are in control. It has taken great persistence on the part of governments and a long-term cultural evolution to embed in us even the basic idea that we should not drink and drive. The hardest thing to change in the quest to improve safety is human behaviour.

Perhaps the most fatalistic point of view comes in the form of the empirical regularity known as Smeed's Law. First proposed by British statistician R. J. Smeed in 1949, Smeed's Law suggests that the number of traffic fatalities can be predicted solely by the number of vehicles registered and the country's population. By his death in 1976, Smeed had shown this held for as many as forty-six countries. No other variables, whether they be improvements in technology or new safety regulations makes any difference. A Model T was as safe to drive as the latest Prius.

Smeed himself had a somewhat dark interpretation of this result. He believed that fundamentally human psychology would only accept a certain level of death. If accidents increased beyond this level, drivers would act more safely. If, by contrast, external improvements drove fatalities below this, drivers would instead drive more dangerously, exchanging the new safety measures for more risk.

Imagine you are driving down a wide, well maintained, straight road with good light and concrete barriers protecting you from the pedestrian areas. Naturally you feel safer: you talk to your passengers, fiddle with the radio, maybe even text your friend to say you're running late. The sum total effect of this can be more than enough to overcome the beneficial effect of new safety measures.

Indeed, risk expert John Adams goes further and suggests that even the 1983 making of seat belts compulsory was, at best, redundant. Traffic deaths in the UK had been falling ever since the 1960s – the trend downward actually stalled after the introduction of the new law, and did not resume again to the early 1990s. What is worse, Adams argues that by encouraging drivers to act more dangerously, the law created more risks for cyclists and pedestrians. In 1935 the ratio of pedestrian and cyclist to car occupant fatalities was six to one, but by 1982 it had fallen as low as 0.8. In 1983, however, it jumped 25 per cent to one and did not fall to 0.8 again for another seven years.[125]

The arguments of Smeed and Adams remain relatively controversial. Many transport experts argue that Smeed's Law no longer holds, and that safety regulations have a real effect on saving lives. The UK has one of the world's best records for traffic safety. Nevertheless, almost everyone now accepts that people may act in a more reckless way if they feel safer. Make roads safer and drivers may often drive more dangerously.

One of the biggest trends in road safety today, there-fore, is conversely to make roads appear more dangerous. The late Dutch traffic engineer Hans Monderman became famous for his approach that removed traffic signs and typi-cal road safety features such as speed bumps and chicanes. Instead, Monderman believed in he what called 'psycho-logical road calming'.[126] Instead of segregating drivers from other road users, he believed that drivers should be made more aware that they share the road. By increasing uncer-tainty and forcing drivers to make more use of their own initiative, he believed that he could increase awareness and thus safety. This approach later served as inspiration for the engineers in Kensington High Street, one of London's busi-est roads. By removing 95 per cent of the signs and taking out the guard rails separating pedestrians from the roads, its engineers managed to decrease pedestrian accidents by as much as 60 per cent.[127]

---

125   Adams, 2010
126   Vanderbilt, 2008, p. 193
127   Ibid., p. 202

There is no perfect means of achieving safety. Humans will always take risks, or do the unexpected. What is more, our quest for perfect safety is not without its costs.

How Much is Safety Worth?

In 2006, the magazine *The Economist* ran a humorous column pretending what the in-flight announcement from a fully truthful airline Veritas Airways might sound like:

> Good morning, ladies and gentlemen... At Veritas Airways, your safety is our first priority. Actually, that is not quite true: if it were, our seats would be rear-facing, like those in military aircraft, since they are safer in the event of an emergency landing ... Your life-jacket can be found under your seat, but please do not remove it now. In fact, do not bother to look for it at all. In the event of a landing on water, an unprecedented miracle will have occurred, because in the history of aviation the number of wide-bodied aircraft that have made successful landings on water is zero... The real reason to switch [phones] off is because they interfere with mobile networks on the ground, but somehow that doesn't sound quite so good.[128]

While amusing, the column was a little exaggerated. Backwards facing seats are indeed marginally safer, but as the heroic landing in 2009 of Flight 1549 in the Hudson River by Captain Chesley 'Sully' Sullenberger showed, jets can and do survive water landings. Nevertheless, such occurrences are so rare that one has to wonder if the safety briefing is really the best use of passengers' time.

Imagine if we treated the boarding of trains the same way we treat the boarding of an aeroplane. Trains are after all a far more dangerous method of transport, and, as the

---

128   http://www.economist.com/opinion/PrinterFriendly.cfm?
        story_id=7884654

2004 Madrid train bombing showed, just as susceptible to the horrors of terrorism.

Each time we wanted to board a train, we'd have to arrive at the station two hours early to be led into a special waiting area. If we were lucky, we might get to pass the time with a little shopping. We'd next have to check in, making sure the authorities could keep a proper eye on our travel plans, and to give security the opportunity to scan our luggage for bombs or weapons. We ourselves would have to be scanned in turn, our refreshments taken away. Once upon the train, attendants would instruct us in the best ways to put on our seat belts and demonstrate the brace position in case of derailment.

Would this save lives?

Perhaps it would. It may well prevent a terrorist plot or ensure that a passenger was sitting with his belt done up rather than wandering over to the buffet in the event of a collision.

But in the process it would add so much inconvenience to the railways as to make them not worth the effort.

Despite the rhetoric, in our own lives we often make implicit trade offs between safety and other objectives. We worry that we will lower our chance of head injury if we wear a helmet whilst cycling,[129] but perhaps we are prepared to accept this risk for the pleasure we get from riding the bike without one. It is possible to live your life abstemiously, eating a vegan diet and never indulging in pleasures or risky sports – but most of would rather enjoy the life with all its risk, rather than living isolated, sheltered lives.

Unfortunately, as difficult emotionally as it might be, we need to take similar decisions over questions about safety as a society.

---

129 The evidence on this isn't absolutely clear cut. Again, some experts suspect that as cyclists with helmets feel safer they in turn cycle more dangerously.

As a country, we too have a choice to make between trying to avoid all risk and a society where we might push forward and achieve more.

Moreover, there is more than one way to save a life. Money we spend installing seatbelts on trains is money that we don't spend on putting better airbags into cars, developing new medical treatments or sending aid to the starving in the developing world.

If we have a fixed budget that we can spend on safety, then it makes sense to spend that money as efficiently as possible on those improvements that are likely to save the most lives for the limited resources that we have.

The only fair and consistent way to measure this in the long run is to use prices. As difficult as it may be emotionally, the only rational way to make decisions is to place a value on a human life. If one proposal saves lives at £500 a time, and the second costs £1000, then clearly it is better to use our money on the first option.

In order to make such decisions, the government uses a rather ugly sounding number, known as the Value per Prevent Fatality (VPF). If an investment will save one life and it is cheaper than the VPF then it is probably worth proceeding with, if it is more expensive we estimate we can better make use of resources elsewhere.

Unfortunately, the government is not consistent with the value it gives to the VPF. In the railways it sets it as high as £3.2m, but on the roads it can be as low as £100,000.[130] You might think that this shows a greater concern for safety in the railways and that this is a good thing, but what it really implies is that we can save thirty-two times as many lives by putting more investment into the roads as we do on rail.

The railways are in fact extraordinarily safe at the moment, enjoying a record far superior to the popular impression that still exists in the wake of the Hatfield rail

130   Wolmar, Christian, *On the Wrong Line*, 2005, p. 239

crash. Like most investments, putting extra money into safety eventually brings diminishing returns. It becomes harder and more expensive to save every extra life.

The truth is that we long ago reached the point of diminishing returns in the rail sector. Costs in the railway lines have grown massively, but we are getting little back for the amount we spend. We can make better use of the money elsewhere.

Knowing What You Do…?

Imagine that a genie gives you a choice: to travel back in time, and put a horrendously dangerous technology back in its box. Not nuclear power or bombs – but the internal combustion engine.

By stopping the car from ever being developed, or becoming an integral part of our society, you can prevent millions of deaths. Each year, more people die in the United States from traffic accidents than were killed in the September 11 attacks.[131]

Knowing all that you know now, would you have stopped cars?

Transport has always been dangerous. The early railways suffered frequent accidents, and there was a horrific rate of injury for the underpaid workers as competing railway companies tried to press on with ever more speed – but then industrial accidents were rife all over the Victorian world.

Early cars were not much safer, and untrained Victorian drivers caused chaos on sleepy English roads. Road rage is by no means a new phenomenon – Kenneth Grahame's Toad of Toad Hall was by no means the only wealthy, dangerous driver at the turn of the century. Despite a 20 mph speed limit and very little traffic, three times as many children were killed by cars in 1922 as were killed by cars in 2008.[132]

---

131   Vanderbilt, 2008, p. 271
132   http://www.john-adams.co.uk/2009/11/05/seat-belts-another-look-at-the-data/

These days cars, trains and even space rockets are much less likely to end in a fatal accident than they once were. But there seems to be an inevitable pattern that in the early days all transport methods have their risks as people struggle to learn how to use them.

Despite all the cost and the pain and the death, it is difficult for all but the most passionate of rail fanatics to really wish away the invention of cars. They have caused death, but also mobility, freedom and wealth. Every day we are given the choice of whether to take the risk of the car or pursue some other transport route, and most of us turn the key in the ignition.

But if the lesson from history is that sometimes progress is worth taking risks, then we have to be worried about the prospects for future technologies.

The Cost of Safety

It may surprise you to know the technology for building a flying car has long existed.

The engineering is the easy part – far harder is making a vehicle both that customers will want to buy, and that will pass the approval of government regulators. As Carl Dietrich, of the start-up Terrafugia Transition is rapidly discovering, it is not easy to please both the regulators for safety in the road and the air. Already he has to fight hard to win exemptions from rules designed for cars or planes – but there remain hundreds of other check boxes he must tick, from the provision of adequate airbags to the height of the bumper.[133]

It is a probably a good thing that regulators keep an eye on new development. After all, the technology for nuclear powered trains or even cars has also long existed, but that does not mean it is necessarily a good idea to bring them to market.

---

133   http://www.slate.com/id/2287738/pagenum/all/#p2

Nevertheless, there is a real danger of a 'chilling effect' on innovation from too many rules designed for different, older technologies. As we will see later on, the technology of self driven computer controlled cars is rapidly making progress. Their current biggest difficulty is arguably not the technological hurdles that have to be overcome, but the risk from liability when things go wrong.

As we will see, the cars are likely to improve safety, but no technology is perfect. New methods of transport often have teething pains, and in our current litigious society these costs are likely to prove enormously costly to any innovator. This might not stop progress – but it could significantly slow it down. We shouldn't forget the lesson of the Victorians, where government regulation in Britain over steam cars stopped all progress on the technology for decades.

Whenever a technology has had to go directly through government, it has often been killed off. Take London's Cycle Hire Scheme, the 'Boris Bikes'. The early results show that the system has been a success and is likely to be profitable. This is exactly the kind of initiative that should have been launched by the private sector, but a private firm would have struggled to get all the necessary planning permission to build the bike stations.

We are a more risk averse society than the Victorians. Life is less cheap – and this is a good thing.

But it does mean that the first time a computer controlled car skids off the road and crushes into a pensioner walking down the pavement, there will be outrage and panic in the media. Even if self driven cars meet the incredible (initial) burden of being safer than our current manual cars, that could still present dozens of stories of accidents for the press to latch onto everyday.

If the Wright brothers were sued every time there was an early plane accident, it is possible we would never have seen the 747. In order to protect new inventors, we need to look into the possibility of giving additional liability cover to vehicle manufacturers. Beyond this, in many places it is actually technically illegal even to experiment with new vehicles such as computer controlled cars on public roads. Big technology companies such as Google have the funds to lobby for changes in the law if they have to – but progress would proceed a lot more smoothly if they didn't have to.

Our greater concern for safety in the modern world is a credit to our society. But there is only so much that you can plan. Accidents and crime will happen, and the unknown and unpredictable will overwhelm the best of procedures. The safer we make humans beings feel, the more they may compensate by taking more reckless risks. We shouldn't let an over-obsession with safety get in the way of new technological developments. A plan for perfect safety is no plan at all, and has real costs in terms of the obstacles it presents for progress.

PART THREE

WHERE WE NEED TO BE

COMMUTING

It was a hot balmy day on a busy road in the middle of Beijing. So busy in fact that traffic had ground to a halt.

Bored drivers tapped their fingers on the dashboard to pass the time. Horns blared. Enterprising hawkers rode up on bikes to sell overpriced food to hungry passengers.

It could have been a traffic jam anywhere in the world, except for one small detail. This traffic jam had been carrying on for ten days. China is a country used to taking things to a scale unprecedented elsewhere, but even this was surprising.

A combination of heavy traffic, road works and breakdowns had all come together in the middle of a hot August day, in a city that by some reports is adding 2,000 cars to the road a day.[134] Slowly the wave of gridlock had grown and extended, until nearly 60 km of motorway had come to a complete halt. Passengers were stranded in their vehicles for days on their own, living off what food and water they could buy and having to be vigilant at night for the roaming thieves looking for easy pickings.

While it sounds like something out of a science fiction film, the traffic jam actually occurred in August 2010.

Is this the future, the way all big cities are heading? Have cars reached the end of their usefulness?

The Civil War in Transport
Strangely, the biggest divide in transport circles is not over questions of taxation or spending, but over what seems to be little more than a matter of taste.

---

134   http://www.thehindu.com/news/international/article592015.ece

In the nineteenth century, new technologies like buses, the Underground and elevators allowed people to live in ever more dense cities. It seemed that in the future every city would look much like New York: ordinary families living in tall residential buildings, and travelling in to work on public transit systems.

In the twentieth century, this trend abruptly came to a halt. Rather than grow up, cities started to spread out, as passengers left behind the bus and tram, driving their own cars to work. Tall, dense cities like New York and London began to look more like a relic from the past than a model to be emulated.

The causes of this change have been a source of argument ever since. Was it a natural result technological and social progression, or a sinister manipulation by corporate and government influences? Should we welcome it as a positive change, allowing ordinary families to enjoy more spacious homes and peaceful neighbourhoods? Or has it caused the hollowing out of our cities, massively increasing social alienation and carbon emissions.

For many years, activists and experts interested in transport have fallen into one of two camps.

One side welcomes the rise of the car and the move out to the suburbs. This, they argue, is how people have chosen to live over the last few decades whenever they can afford it or there is enough land. People expect to live in a comfortable property with a spacious garden, residing in a safe, quiet neighbour away from the crime and noise of the city. When they need to travel, they can make use of their own car to get wherever they need.

While it is true that cars rely on roads built by the government, they say, this is more than compensated for by the taxes drivers pay. We should stop the current 'war on the motorist', and let people use the transport methods they prefer. Our transport infrastructure and land planning systems should be optimised to create as free flowing systems of traffic as possible.

And then there is the opposing camp, the urbanist Planners who prefer public transport and city living. These Urbanists believe that rather than letting our lives be taken over by the car, we should instead follow the principles of 'smart growth', looking to make our communities as socially and environmentally sustainable as possible. Their ideal is a neighbourhood where you can walk by foot to your local bar or shop, with an extensive system of public transit to take you into work. We should all swap our cars for a bike and Oyster card.

To these urbanists, our current car-dependent system of living is far from natural. They argue that drivers currently do not pay nearly enough to cover the pollution and health dangers their vehicles create. Moreover, cars are only preferred because of the enormous implicit subsidies from a century-old tradition of government-provided roads. Some urbanists go even further than this – according to them, our nineteenth century transit-based economy was killed off by a conspiracy of government and automobile manufacturers. According to the 'Greet Streetcar Scandal' (dramatised in, of all things, the family film *Who Killed Roger Rabbit?*), companies such as General Motors deliberately bought up and shut down the remaining tram and train services, to clear the way for their four-wheeled vehicles.

The two sides often act as the mirror image of each other. When one argues for enforced parking minimums, the other argues for parking maximums. One side argues that traffic problems can only be solved by building more roads; the other that new roads will only cause even more traffic. One argues about the extensive subsidies given to public transport over the years; the other about the subsides given to cars.

The war between the urbanists and the road enthusiasts has many fronts. In the next chapter we'll examine the 'war on the motorist' and the Planners' attempts to move us away from the motorways onto trains and other forms of public transport.

But first we'll look closer at the arguments over what at first seems to be such a simple question: how should we get to work?

How Should You Get to Work?

Whether you take the car, train or bus into work may at first seem a minor issue, but behind it lie some very fundamental issues over how we want to live. What sort of environment do we want to live in and who should decide? How should we all get to work, school or the shops? Should communities be forcibly intermingled, or should we allow them to become ever more segregated?

In other words, the impacts of our transport choice aren't just economic. They also affect our environment and our communities, our struggles with crime and inequality, and the way we all go about our daily routine.

But just because such decisions have such big impacts, that doesn't necessarily make them the responsibility of governments to control or change. The choice of what community we want to live in is an intensely personal one. The job of government is to expand our range of options, not to constrict it.

The most visible effect of changing transport technology can be seen in the geography of our cities. As technological progress continues, the range one can travel from work to home in a reasonable time grows, and consequently, so does the size of the city itself. Cities grow like trees, as new outer rings are added over times with the progress of technology.

Take the example of London.

At first, workers would get to work using the most traditional method of their own two feet. In their thousands, they crossed the Thames and made their way to work, filling the city streets.

Then came the stagecoaches and omnibuses, long carriages drawn by horses that could carry as many as eighteen people at once. By foot, a worker can only cover around 1.5 miles in the typical half-hour commute, while omnibuses could double this range.[135]

These innovations slowly expanded the borders of the city, but the real push came with the development of trams and the new Underground train network in London. Everywhere the new Tube lines sprung out, new housing developments rapidly followed in their wake. Former peaceful country towns such as Rickmansworth quickly became subsumed into the wider metropolis.

As our cities and urban environments become ever more dense, the methods workers use to commute will matter ever more. Most of us have had to suffer the stress and frustration of the daily drive in to work, waiting through traffic, longing to get home. Indeed, the compounding misery caused by too long a commute seems far out of proportion with the time it takes. Expert researchers suggested that someone with an hour-long commute in each direction has to earn an extra 40 per cent to be as happy as his colleague who walks to the office.[136]

But beyond this, as we've already discussed in Chapter 3, in many ways cities are the future of our economy. The denser and bigger our cities grow, the richer we become. However, cities also offer unique challenges for new infrastructure as well. The more people we try to pack together in a close space, the harder it becomes to transport them all efficiently to where they need to go. It also becomes more expensive, as the extra value the workers create drives up the value of land.

So, how do we make the transport systems of our cities work better?

---

135 Glaesar, 2011, p. 169

136 Alois Stutzer & Bruno S. Frey, 'Stress That Doesn't Pay: The Commuting Paradox,' IEW - Working Papers iewwp151, Institute for Empirical Research in Economics

Why do We Get Traffic Jams?

When investigating transport, the problems of queuing and congestion rapidly become familiar. There is simply not enough space for all the drivers who want to use a road, or airlines who want to use an airport. Queuing acts as a rationing system for the limited supply available, just as shoppers had to queue for limited food in wartime.

It is worth realising that this isn't a natural state of affairs. The long traffic jams we may be forced to endure on our daily commute don't just happen – they are the result of two key failings of governments.

The first necessary condition is limited supply. Sometimes, this limited supply is the sad result of geography or physics. There are only so many roads that you can fit inside a city, or planes that can safely land at the same time.

But just as often this lack of supply is the fault of the government. Whether for political or budgetary reasons it has decided not to build any more capacity, as in the choice governments of both parties have made largely to stop building roads since the early 1990s. In other cases the government has made it very difficult with overly bureaucratic regulations for private developers to create their own facilities. We're left with what the government will provide for us, and often, this simply isn't enough.

Limited supply isn't enough on its own to cause queuing. At some margin, there is limited supply of most physical goods in our economy. There are only so many hotels in the world, so many TVs or so many chocolate bars. Nevertheless, most of us manage to find a hotel room, new TV or snack whenever we need one.

The second condition that creates queuing is when prices aren't allowed to adjust. When a new iPhone comes out, Apple won't let you pay more and skip the queue to get it first. Many exclusive restaurants are massively over-subscribed, but prefer to keep prices down and force you to wait months to obtain a table. We don't let you pay more to jump the queue for a kidney donation. In each case, instead of rationing by price, we ration by time.

In transport, it is often the government that forces prices to stay still. Regulators put strict limits on the maximum prices railway and aviation companies may charge, no matter how full their trains or airports may get.

When the government owns the infrastructure itself, there may simply be no prices to change in the first place. Aside from a few isolated exceptions, you can drive on any road in the country without paying any charge. While nobody likes spending more money, the result of this is that we often waste large proportions of our time in traffic jams and congestion.

Perhaps you might argue that although congestion is frustrating, at least queuing is a fair system. Poor and rich alike have to wait their turn while stuck in a traffic jam. If we introduced a new system of pricing for roads it might give the wealthy driver a more pleasant journey, but force all the less well off motorists off the roads.

But it turns out that in practice this doesn't seem to happen. Several states in the US have already experimented with road pricing on special 'Lexus Lanes'. What they've discovered is not only are the lanes highly popular once in place, but that the majority of the users aren't wealthy at all.[137] The rich do tend us to use the new lanes more, but only marginally so. After all, the rich tend to go to expensive restaurants and on exotic holidays more often as well, but all of us occasionally splash out. Sometimes we all find that it is worth spending a little money to save a lot of time. Interestingly, a far more important determinant of using the special lanes than wealth is gender: women are 10 per cent more likely to use them.[138]

---

137   http://www.freakonomics.com/2009/01/08/why-youll-love-paying-for-roads-that-used-to-be-free-part-two/

138   Edward Sullivan, Continuation Study to Evaluate the Impacts of the SR 91 Value-Priced Express Lanes, December 2000 http://ceenve3.civeng.calpoly.edu/sullivan/SR91/final_rpt/FinalRep2000.pdf

Congestion Charging, Now and Then

If you overlay a map of London's old turnpike roads over the top of today's Congestion Charging zone, you find a remarkable spatial match between the two.[139] London, like all big cities, has always faced problems with traffic and experimented with different means to try and tame it.

For hundreds of years, London's authorities have struggled to deal with the problem of packing too many people into too few streets. In medieval times, they tried to restrict the hours that drivers could come into the town. In Victorian times, they constructed a massive new Underground network. In the twenty-first century, we've introduced a Congestion Charge.

Indeed, the problem of urban congestion on the roads is at least as old as the Roman Empire, which frequently suffered the eternal traffic conundrum of too many chariot drivers trying to pack into too few narrow Roman streets. In response, they made use of traffic calming measures, pedestrianised central squares, and introduced one-way streets. Julius Caesar became so frustrated at the congestion in Rome that he banned non essential vehicles from the streets before 3 p.m. Unfortunately, pushing traffic into the night had the regrettable side effect of making it much harder to sleep.[140]

The fact that the problem is so long lived is one clue that it won't be solved by any new piece of infrastructure. It should make us pause that before Crossrail, before the Jubilee Line extension, before the Underground and buses, before the automobile and tram, London still suffered from traffic jams. Improving infrastructure is good for many reasons, but it won't reduce traffic jams in the long term on its own.

---

139   You can see for yourself at http://spatialanalysis.co.uk/2010/12/
      05/18th-century-congestion-charging/

140   For an entertaining look at other historical examples of traffic chaos,
      Tom Vanderbilt's *Traffic* (Penguin, 2008) is an excellent resource.

As cities grow in their importance to our economy, we're going to continue to see more demand that can be met within the constrained limits of city roads. To tackle the problem we will have to manage demand rather than supply. That's why governments across the world have begun to seriously investigate new road pricing systems, such as congestion charges.

So, has the London Congestion Charge been a success?

It certainly seems that way. In international academia, London is often pointed to alongside Stockholm and Singapore as an example of how to tackle congestion. Although initially unpopular with London residents, it has now been grudgingly accepted. The first few years of the policy seemed to show a marked decrease in traffic on London streets, although some claim that a significant contribution to this was a simultaneous halt to road works. No politician seriously suggests removing the charge, and it is popular with policy wonks of all political persuasions.

And yet, the system monitoring drivers is extraordinarily expensive to run, with operating costs nearly half the revenue raised.[141] Economists Rémy Prud'homme and Juan Pablo Bocarejo estimate that once you've including operating costs and amortisation of the initial capital that the scheme only produces benefits worth €104m a year, compared to €177m in costs.[142]

Traffic levels have continued to climb, until the point that they are now back at the same levels as before the introduction of the charge.

Now, the fact that we are back where we started does not necessarily mean that the scheme has been a failure. We don't know what would happen in an alternative scenario where traffic levels were allowed to rise without hindrance.

---

141   Bowerman, 2007
142   Prud'homme, 2004

But it does suggest that there is room for improvement in the way the Charge works. The first country to implement a congestion charge was Singapore, and in many ways the latest evolution of their system shows the way forward. Singapore replaced its flat rate Area Licensing Scheme with a new Electronic Road Pricing scheme in 1998. Under this scheme, a varying price can be adjusted easily for location and time, and is displayed directly to the driver through a small gadget attached to the windscreen. In 2006, the Singaporean authorities ran further tests in association with IBM to experiment with the possibilities of variable pricing, dynamically lowering or raising costs to minimise congestion at all times.

Similarly, we should look into making our own system more finely grained. At the moment, the Charge as a whole is a crude instrument. In a perfect world of course we would vary the price for each road for each hour of the day. Even if that is unfeasible, we could do a lot better by charging more for peak times and peak roads. The second and easiest change would to raise the price. Since the system's introduction, we've seen prices only rise from £5 to £10.

It is important, of course, to be clear what the aim of the charge is – to keep traffic moving smoothly – and limit it to those situations where it can be best used. No matter how sophisticated, no system of pricing would allow all London's residents to drive to work.

For that task, we will need to turn to the Tube.

The Problem of the Underground
The arguments between urbanists and car enthusiasts have often lined up on a familiar left–right partisan divide. No doubt a large reason for this is that cars are seen as a free market, a privatised and individualistic form of transport in comparison to often government owned, public forms of transport.

In many ways, however, this left–right divide is mislead-ing. No other form of transport after all, is as socialistic as our road system, a public service free at the point of use and completely government controlled. By contrast, in their nineteenth-century heyday, transit systems such as London's Underground or American street cars were devel-oped by private sector entrepreneurs. It was only later that government stepped in and took over their operation.

That said, just because industries were previously under the control of private sector control does not mean we can easily return them back to private control.

The example of New Labour's Public Private Partnership on the Underground provides a sad fable about the limits of planning.

Throughout its history, the story of the Underground has reflected the main railway system. Originally created in a burst of private sector innovation in the mid nine-teenth century, in the wake of its success it proceeded in rapid if haphazard fashion to extend its network, until by the early twentieth century it spread across the capi-tal. Nationalised as a strategic asset in the 1930s, the network suffered in the post-war decades from under investment and from incompetent management. Those new projects that were launched, such as the Jubilee Line extension, inevitably overran their allotted time and budget.

Under the leadership of John Prescott, the New Labour administration of the late 1990s committed itself to no more transport privatisation, but this did not remove the need for extensive new investment in the Underground. The Treasury was, as ever, unwilling to sign a blank cheque, and had no confidence in the public sector's ability to control costs.

Thus the compromise that was the Public Private Partnership. The term in itself was deliberately vague, seemingly chosen only as an attempt to distinguish the concept from Public Finance Initiatives. No definition of the differences between the two was ever given, and official documents often seem to use the two interchangeably.

In a mirror of the structural changes undertaken on the main lines, the Underground's operations were maintained in the public sector while infrastructure investment was to be handled by two private consortia, later called Tube Lines and Metronet. The division was to be determined by time – the public sector would run the lines during the day, but at night, or during the weekend, the private sector would then perform essential maintenance and renewal work. These initial contracts were to be signed for a thirty-year period, in order to give the private sector operator the maximum time necessary to recoup the advantages of its investments.

This structure, it was believed, would have multiple benefits. The management of the London Underground would be sidelined, and the Underground would enjoy the benefits of private sector managerial efficiency and innovation. The private sector would put forward the initial funds, allowing extensive amounts to be borrowed off the government's balance sheet. Almost as crucially, this financing would have long-term stability, rather than the stop-start manner in which much public finance was usually distributed.

But then the downsides of this structure were likewise familiar.

While the new structure would certainly raise more initial money, eventually all this money would have to be paid for, now with a profit margin attached. There was no free lunch, only an accounting trick. This borrowing would have to take place on private sector terms, rather than enjoy the lower interest rates that government could enjoy. There would have to be significant new efficiencies achieved by the private sector in order to compensate for these additional costs.

And then there was the problem of transferring risk, familiar from the problems of rail franchising. There existed the usual dilemma of integrating sufficient incentives into the system, while not paying enormous amounts simply to cover risks that the contractors could not control.

The government decided to rely on an array of targets to tackle this dilemma. The contracts for the PPP quickly became enormous, volume upon volume dictating exactly when and where everything had to be replaced, how much everything should cost and how long it all should take to build. Such a bureaucratic apparatus may have given the feeling of control, but it pitted the public sector against the private in a series of endless arguments about the cost and direction of every procedure. No contract could ever hope to spell out every contingency in detail.

Initially granted control in 2003, by 2008 the new company Metronet was facing severe financial difficulties and had to be put into administration. The government attempted to find a new PPP partner without much success, and by 2010, when Tube Lines faced a similar funding shortfall, Transport for London quickly arranged a buyout, returning the Underground back into public hands. It is difficult to think of many policies that have so comprehensively failed in such a short time.

The bill for this downfall was enormous. The entire structure had cost nearly £500m in consultancy fees just to set up. On no account could the project be described as a success, but the new operators had succeeded in improving efficiency in some areas, such as maintenance and repair. Those who were ideologically opposed to any private sector involvement will no doubt put any success down to the high level of new investment flowing into the railway, but the matter remains that by many criteria the Underground was improving, albeit at unacceptably high levels of cost and delay.

While the project was flawed and likely destined to failure from its inception, it did at least have the merits of introducing some accountability into a public sector that had been allowed to stagnate for fifty years. Although not a solution for everything, private sector management did introduce reform and improvements.

There is no real evidence that the private sector's original running of the network was inefficient, and much to suggest otherwise, but a full privatisation of the Underground would now prove politically and logistically difficult. It is not clear how the network could be divided, or how to avoid the problems of monopoly since, in a congested network such as London, the Underground would enjoy in effect an overwhelmingly powerful position. Neither would it be possible to avoid government interference if subsidy was needed to fund new lines.

What is clear is the repetition of lessons we have seen elsewhere. There is no perfect solution to the general problem of interactions between the public and private sectors. Government cannot plan the future, no matter how detailed its plans or the number of its targets. Creating a new competitive market is difficult.

Nevertheless, while structural reform may have proved difficult, the Underground is too important to the future of London to be left entirely alone. Continuing to improve and expand the network remains a priority as London continues to grow. The rest of the country understandably can get annoyed when London receives such a large proportion of the country's investment funds, but there is no real reason for this money to come out of the central budget. Instead the city will likely have more autonomy and be able to grow faster if it raises more of its own funds, perhaps through the already discussed innovative funding methods being used for the current Northern line extension.

New Labour's PPP might have failed, but the need for further investment certainly hasn't gone away.

Planning Our Cities

If we are honest, we have less ability to shape the future path of our cities than sometimes we like to admit. Cities that were once seen in long-term decline such as London and New York have come back into health. Other industrial areas such as Detroit or England's North have struggled to find a new function. A city is closer to an organic entity that has to be nurtured than a factory that can be architected and designed.

If we can't plan the future of our cities, then we will never be able to plan perfectly their transport needs. In the mid twentieth century new cities such as Milton Keynes in England or Chandigarh in India were designed around car-centred living. They have not always been aesthetically popular, but then the record of new transit schemes has been less than ideal as well. Schemes such as the Edinburgh Tram or Cambridge Busway have run vastly over budget and over schedule.

The current partisan war between public and private transport is unhelpful. As we have seen in this chapter, both road and rail have their problems. We need to improve both, rather than try to dictate from the centre how people ought to live.

That means easing up on the control our land planning system has on the type of residential or commercial buildings that can be built. It means getting rid both of regulation that enforces parking maximums and parking minimums. It means making it easier to provide both new roads and new bus services. The government's job is to provide a level playing field.

These days indeed, cities probably need a far greater range of transport options than can be provided by the traditional trio of car, bus and train.

The newest entrant, of course, is the Barclays Cycle Hire scheme. More informally known as the 'Boris Bikes' initiative, this scheme provides 'pick up and go' bikes from a network of stations across the city. Alternatively, perhaps we could make better use of the water at the heart of the city. In their 2009 report *At a Rate of Knots*, the think tank Policy Exchange suggests that we are not fully utilising the potential of the Thames as a means of transportation to carry passengers across London. This could be done at very little expense, and help to cut down congestion in the city centre.

As technology progresses we are likely to see less reliance on a single method of transport, and a wider variety of modes. Rather than try to plan the exact shape of our cities, we should free up regulation, planning and local authorities to allow a far wider degree of experimentation. As we will see in the last chapter, entrepreneurs are already working on a vast array of new and varied ways of getting around the city.

In large cities such as London, privately driven cars will likely see relative decline in the future. The Tubes and buses carry the majority of the traffic, while cars and taxis carry urgent or emergency passengers. The European Union has already called for a ban on petrol-driven cars in city centres by 2050.[143]

But then London is a special case. Extensive transit systems might eventually be necessary for large cities such as Birmingham or Manchester, but do we really want to create extensive systems of Underground railway lines in Exeter or Northampton? At some point, it will be easier to rely on cars than pay the expensive costs to install train and other transit systems.

That is, of course, if cars have a place in our future transport mix at all?

---

143   http://www.bbc.co.uk/news/uk-politics-12879566

ROADS

If you happened to be wandering the rural roads of Wales in 1840, you might have chanced to come upon a very strange sight.

A group of male farmers, all dressed in women's clothing, clubs ready in hand.

The leader of the group would call out: 'What is this my children? There is something in my way. I cannot go on.'

His followers would reply: 'What is it, mother Rebecca? Nothing should stand in your way?'

Feigning confusion the leader would say: 'I do not know my children. I am old and cannot see well.'

After a few more rounds of this pantomime, they would finally get to the climax of their performance, as the leader would despair, 'Oh my dear children, it is locked and bolted. What can be done?'

Somewhat chillingly the mob would reply, 'It must be taken down, mother. You and your children must be able to pass.'

At which point the leader would proclaim, 'Off with it then, my children,'[144] and the destruction would begin.

These were not easy years for local rural communities. A serious of unfortunate harvests had led to the prices of their crops falling, while rents and taxes remained as high as ever. Angry about their newfound poverty the farmers chose one particular symbol of their believed oppression on which to take out their anger: the tollgate.

---

144 http://www.southwalespolicemuseum.org.uk/en/content/cms/
    visit_the_archives/the_rebecca_riots/the_rebecca_riots.aspx

Bands of Welsh farmers roamed the countryside, destroying tollgates where they found them. They called themselves the Rebecca rioters, perhaps in reference to the biblical verse Genesis 24:60 – 'And they blessed Rebekah and said unto her, Thou art our sister, be thou the mother of thousands of millions, and let thy seed possess the gate of those which hate them.'

By 1843 the riots had come to an end, and in 1844 the Turnpikes Act was passed in Parliament, simplifying and lowering the rates.

But the Rebecca riots were hardly to be the last occasion in which drivers protested against a perceived government imposition. Road pricing, it seems, has never been popular.

The War on the Motorist

It can be easy to persuade oneself that there is a war on the motorist.

Government transport policy, when it even bothers to mention the roads, seems like a long list of new restrictions and attacks: new speed cameras, checks for drink driving, stricter driving tests, road bumps, road narrowing, congestion charges, taxes, fuel duty increases, vehicle duty bands, lower speed limits.

Not surprisingly, whenever governments have dared to mention it, the idea of road pricing has been unpopular. Yet another tax? More bureaucracy? Another deprivation of our privacy? Can't we just have more roads instead?

But then urbanist Planners remain fierce opponents of both cars and any further road construction. They argue passionately that building new roads is pointless. Increasing capacity only increases demand – reducing congestion for a few years, but never eliminating it. Moreover, each increase in the traffic on our roads increases the total level of greenhouse gases. The only long-term solution to our traffic problems, these critics argue, is to wean the British public off their addiction to the automobile and onto far more environmentally friendly systems of public transport.

Even the few minor road projects that New Labour announced were too much for some Planners. 'It doesn't grapple with the core of the problem,' complained Professor David Begg, the then chairman of the Commission for Integrated Transport. 'It's a bit like a heroin addict's last fix. It will feel good at the time, but it's not sustainable... At some point you have to lead, because if it's just down to focus groups, why do we have politicians?'[145]

Considering the strength of feeling on both sides, it is no surprise that governments for the last twenty years have chosen to stick to the status quo rather than try politically difficult reform. If there was ever any doubt of the political risk, the 2000 fuel crisis showed the importance of these issues to Middle England and the country at large.

However politically attractive this wait and see approach may be, it will become less and less sustainable as traffic demand and congestion continues to rise. We can't ignore the car forever.

Road Socialism

When you think about, the way we actually run our road system is bizarre. There seems to be no fundamental economic reason that the government should own, operate and offer the road system for free. Whatever arguments could be made for roads could just as easily be made for rail – and even the most fervent supporters of rail nationalisation do not believe that you should be able to board a train without first buying a ticket.

For whatever reason roads have joined alongside primary education, health and police the select list of goods that government provides for free. While the government is

---

happy to let us pay for our food, water and heating, roads it seems are just too important to be left to the market. As libertarian a thinker as Milton Friedman admitted that, when it came to driving, he was a 'road socialist.'[146]

There was no deliberate conspiracy by governments or companies such as General Motors to kill off other methods of transport. However, by their actions, governments across the world implicitly subsidised the car, while making it ever harder for services such as rail to compete by imposing strict regulation and limits on the prices rail companies were allowed to charge. It was always going to be hard for transit systems such as intercity train services to remain viable when the government was undercutting them with a new, free, fast network of national motorways.

Supporters of the roads often argue that, while it may be true that nobody pays for the roads directly, once the taxes drivers pay have been taken into account, they more than cover their own costs. This may be narrowly true in terms of accounting costs, but it misses out on the opportunity costs of the valuable land roads often take up, especially within dense urban areas.

The truth is that there has been no free market in transport for the last hundred years, in either 'public' transport or on the road. Both markets have been massively distorted by government intervention and subsidy. It is impossible to know what different choices as a society we might have made in some alternate world where there was a fair playing field. Perhaps many more of us would live in denser cities, and take public transport into work.

Nevertheless, however we ended up with today's mix of transport, the practical problem is what we can do to make it work better in the future.

---

146 http://marketurbanism.com/2008/08/20/block-on-road-socialism/

The End of the Car?

'Would it have been better if transport technology had atro-
phied at the end of the [nineteenth] century and the car had
never come to dominate the world?' asks transport writer
Christian Wolmar at the end of his book *Blood, Iron and
Gold*. 'Imagine a world without car parks, motorways or
service stations... Think of all those delightful towns and
cities not blighted by the permanent gridlock that affects
them today.'[147]

Indeed, why do we need cars at all, argue the environmentalists? Wouldn't life be better without the pollution,
the accidents and the death? If we can build good enough
systems of public transport, then they would be quite
superfluous. Fast trains can transport us across the country,
while buses take us into work. Aren't pedestrianised urban
areas so much more pleasant? Wouldn't it be nice if the
whole country was like that?

But what would life without a car really be like?

We'd all find it much more difficult to get around,
having to spend more time waiting for buses or rushing to
make the right connection. Mothers bringing up small children would find it much more difficult to leave their home
and go shopping. We'd all live in small cramped houses,
crowded together nearest the railway station to make sure
we could easily commute. It would be, in other words, as if
we all lived in London.

Let's get serious. Cars aren't perfect and there's many
things that they don't do very well, but there are some
advantages that only a car can give you. They are not
simply going to disappear, or ever be completely replaced
by public transport.

A personal car offers privacy and autonomy, the luxury
of being able to choose one's own company. They can be

---

147   Wolmar, *Blood, Iron and Gold: How the Railways Transformed
      the World*, 2009, p. 330

upgraded at will, fitted with the latest comforts or gadgets, allow their owners to express their own personality or fashion whims. Most importantly, they allow the driver to decide exactly when and where he or she wishes to travel, without having to wait or be subject to a timetable.

Understanding the different causes of why we live the way we do is not easy, but we can get some idea from a historical experiment: the different paths the Continent and America chose to take. While America pushed the car, setting down regulations forcing minimum parking spaces and holding down prices on the public railways, Europe took the opposite approach, forcing cars off the road whenever possible and massively subsidising public transport.

It has made little difference. The use of cars in Europe lags only slightly behind that in America. America has 7.76 cars for every ten people, while Italy has six, Germany 5.66 and France five. The gap is still narrowing. Eighty-four per cent of passenger transport by mile in France is done in cars – and this is despite petrol prices five times as high as in the US.[148] As Europeans have grown richer, they've been able to overcome higher taxes and choose with their wallets which technology they prefer.

On the other hand, cars are not perfect for every situation. Driving a car requires high levels of concentration and significant training. In comparison to other travel modes, cars have a terrible safety record. The time travelling cannot be used for other more productive purposes; a business executive driving to London cannot read through his emails in the same manner his counterpart can on the train. They can be environmentally unfriendly and they take up far more land than other modes of transport.

To a large degree, the best method of transport depends on the type of journey. In rural areas, where land is abundant and people scarce, the high operating costs of public

---

148 Glaesar, 2011, p. 178

transport make it impractical. Trying to run train track to every small village in the country would not only be enormously wasteful, but hurtful to the environment as well. On the other hand, in urban areas, where people are abundant and land scarce, it is more natural to think that public transport will be more efficient for the economy and environment.

For journeys of considerable distance between the nation's cities, the calculations become more complex. The convenience of not having to haul luggage through a busy station may be attractive to one consumer, while another prefers the ability to work on a train. The best way to manage such a decision is to let the market and individuals decide for themselves.

In the past, Planners have been able to attack cars as a 'dirty' technology. As new battery technology develops, that may no longer be true in the future. Already, every major car company is competing to get out their latest hybrid and fully electric models. It would not at all be surprising if in a couple of decades we have fully transitioned to carbon-free driving.

The environmental damage isn't the only downside of cars, of course. But, as we will see in the last chapter, new technology threatens to overcome many of these other disadvantages as well. Soon, we will have new models of cars that are more flexible, take up less urban space, have better safety records and even drive themselves.

The fact that all these technological improvements don't seem to have assuaged the Planners' ire against the vehicles suggests that their complaint is as much ideological as pragmatic. While cars will not be the only method of transport we use in the future, they do not look likely to disappear any time soon.

Building More Roads

Britain's roads are already among the most congested in Europe. An estimated 20 per cent of British road users experience congestion compared with just 7 per cent in

Germany and 4 per cent in France.[149] The current level of
infrastructure in Britain simply cannot cope with demand:
in the last twenty-five years, traffic has increased 81 per
cent.[150] The total number of vehicles licensed in the UK has
risen from 25 million in 1995 to 34.1 million in 2010.[151]
This is expected to continue, the distance travelled by car
estimated to increase by 46 per cent through till 2031.[152]

After the war, governments of all persuasions followed
a policy that was known as predict-and-provide. Transport
planners would do their best to predict the numbers and
locations of drivers in the future, and funds for capacity
improvements would be allocated accordingly. We still use
a similar system to decide what funding is needed for new
airport runways or railway lines.

The problem was a phenomenon known as the fundamental law of road congestion. No matter how fast roads
were built, traffic would continue to grow even faster.[153]
New roads might increase the number of drivers on the
road, but they didn't seem to make the roads themselves
less busy. This, it was suggested, meant that building new
roads was a waste of time. As the political costs of building
new roads grew with highly visible environmental protests,
in particular in the early 1990s, politicians realised that it
was easier to simply abandon road building altogether.

But this bleak conclusion doesn't necessarily follow.

Demand for using the roads clearly isn't infinite everywhere – many country roads are lucky to see a dozen or
so travellers a day. In some fantastic world, where we
could fit as many cars as we wanted on a given road, we

---

149   Green Light Group Facts, May 2007
150   Road Pricing, Institute for Mechanical Engineers, p. 10
151   http://www.dft.gov.uk/pgr/statistics/datatablespublications/
      vehicles/licensing/
152   Road Pricing, Institute for Mechanical Engineers, p. 2
153   Duranton, 2009

would eventually reach a limit to new drivers coming onto the roads.

Indeed, the complaint that the creation of more supply only creates further demand is a strange one. Many businesses would welcome such an outcome. Television producers do not complain that the existence of more television channels has resulted in more viewers. From the perspective of society, if people desire frequency and convenience in travel, it is good that we can give it to them.

The problem, of course, is that building a new road has costs as well as benefits. At the moment each additional mile driven on our roads is only a cost to the Treasury, adding to the wear and tear on the road's surface. It provides no additional revenues to pay for the new infrastructure.

There is another way. There is no reason that private companies cannot be responsible for new road projects, or buy already existing trunk roads.

Although an unusual experience to the British, the experience of paying tolls for motorways is well established practice on the Continent and in the US. We could build on the largely successful experiment of Birmingham's M6 toll road[154] and invite bidders for other key transport projects that public money cannot currently support. Although much derided in the press, private financial initiatives seem to have performed well in the road industry, as estimates have suggested that they achieved savings of between 14 per cent and 22 per cent in their first eight projects.[155]

While building more roads can't by itself solve the problems of congestion, especially within crowded city centres there are other locations where new trunk roads could improve the flow of traffic or ease pressure on other roads.

---

154 Despite disappointing user numbers, the project succeeded in adding new road capacity at minimal cost to the Exchequer.

155 Richard Wellings and Briar Lipson, Towards better transport, Policy Exchange, 2008, p. 6

New roads have as just much potential to boost economic growth as new railway connections. In their report *Towards Better Transport* Richard Wellings and Briar Lipson suggest that

> There are still obvious gaps in the network; Manchester and Sheffield, two of the country's largest cities and only thirty miles apart, have no direct motorway connection... There is no link between Newcastle and Edinburgh or Newcastle and Glasgow, and the current A1 link follows an indirect and time-consuming route... The large conurbations of the North East of England (Teesside and Tyneside) have yet to be linked to the main motorway network.[156]

Many benefits would come from breaking up the government's monopoly on road building. Private investors can access new funds outside general government borrowing. They can experiment with new ideas. To some degree, they can avoid many of the difficult political issues.

Ultimately, however, sadly no road building programme is likely to be fast enough under the current political realities to cope with increasing demand. Greater rationing, whether by price or, by default, queuing, is an inevitability.

The Cost of Free Roads

The cost of congestion is no small matter. Recent estimates suggest that we waste around £10bn every year from time stuck in traffic. The government's Eddington Review of Britain's transport system concluded that this could rise to be as much as £22bn by 2024.[157]

Congestion is bad for the environment as well. Cars sitting idle in traffic still produce high levels of damaging greenhouse gases.

---

156 Wellings & Lipson, 2008, p. 10
157 Road Pricing, Institute for Mechanical Engineers, p. 2

The principal reason this congestion exists is because drivers get to use the roads for free.

Imagine if all taxis were nationalised and provided for free. No doubt we would all find many new excuses to use taxis, and suddenly find indispensable what before we had done without. Even if the queues at taxi ranks continued to grow, many of us would rather put up with this than suffer the bus or tube.

Any resource will be used more than it should be if imperfections in the market mean that its price is lower than it really costs. But the problem gets even worse when the good is entirely free, for reasons as much of psychology as economics.

Marketers have long understood that customers do not respond rationally to a free good. The psychological gap between free and any price at all – the 'penny gap' as some have called it – is enormous. Consumers will happily gorge on freebies that they would disdain if they cost only a few pennies. The importance of this difference can be seen in the struggles the newspaper industry has faced in its attempts to get customers to accept micropayments for its content.

But if the problem we face is well known, so is the solution. For over fifty years, economists and politicians have been preaching the advantages of introducing new systems of road pricing.

The principle of road pricing is hardly unprecedented. As we've seen, eighteenth century turnpike roads helped to modernise Britain's medieval infrastructure. It's familiar internationally, long having been used for sections of the motorway on the Continent and the US. It's even a familiar experience in the UK today. Drivers are now used to paying for entering London in peak hours, for travelling along the M6 toll road or crossing the Severn Bridge.

Ever since the old turnpike lanes disappeared, the government has occasionally looked at the possibility of reintroducing a new such system.

For example, in 1967 the Prime Minister, Harold Wilson, expressed an interest in the turnpike concept in internal meetings.[158] This it was hoped might be able to fund construction of further motorways without any direct cost to the Exchequer. Although the idea was never taken very seriously, the sceptical Civil Service did take the trouble to construct a careful briefing on the proposals.

The then Secretary of State for Transport, Barbara Castle, was if anything even more opposed to the idea, believing that even the briefing was a waste of time. In a private letter to Jack Diamond, Chief Secretary of the Treasury, she wrote, 'the arguments, both of principle and practice, against any such project seem to me to be overwhelming.'[159]

It is interesting however to look at exactly what the arguments against the proposals were. The biggest concern shared by Castle and her civil servants was that 'the cost of collecting the tolls would be very high'.[160] At the time, any new system of tolls would have required extensive investment and ongoing costs to build and man a new series of toll-booths. These booths in turn would act as a severe hindrance to traffic, slowing it down and pushing drivers away onto other already more congested roads. Besides, at the time, the UK government was still steadily expanding the motorways year on year. The marginal extra expansion of the network that would be added by new toll roads did not seem worth either the logistical or the political costs.

But the Civil Service was prescient enough to know that these problems would not always exist. What was needed the civil servants decided, was 'some device, not too heavy, bulky or expensive which will record the mileage run over certain roads, and which cannot be tampered with.'[161]

---

158   Letter from I. H. Lightman to Vinter , 1967
159   Letter from Barbara Castle to John Diamond, 1967
160   Ibid.
161   McKean, 1969

Such a device of course now does exist. Most of us carry around one in our mobile phones.

The most direct advantage of road pricing we've already discussed: rationing road space by price is far more efficient than rationing it by queuing. But there are other benefits as well. Putting some price on roads stops them being seen as a 'free' good, and all the strange psychological effects this can create. It would put a limit on the demand that Planners claim is insatiable.

Road pricing helps internalise some of the problems Planners claim excess traffic causes, and gives impetus to society to investigate other ideas. Is it really necessary that the entire working population tries to commute within the same two narrow rush hours? Would be it possible to start to stagger office hours? Does every office need to be in the centre of a city, or could some be located in the suburbs?

Beyond this, road pricing would help us reform the whole system of roads. It gives a better sense of exactly which journeys drivers find essential, and which they are only making as it is free. This not only makes it much easier for governments to plan future capacity improvements, but gives a better sense to the private sector of the commercial return it might make in its own programme of road construction. If a new pricing system works as it should, then new roads can quickly pay back for themselves.

As the Civil Service argued back in 1967, tolling can be used both 'in the interests of the reduction of congestion [and] as a guide to road construction priorities.'[162] Back then, the technology was still so basic that 'we can [not] usefully pursue this any further in the immediate future; in the long term, the case may need to be looked at again.'[163]

But if the solution to our ever growing congestion problem has long been understood, and the technological

---

162   Letter from R. C. W. Cox to Downey , 1967
163   Ibid.

challenges keep getting easier, as a country we seem to be further away from introducing road pricing than ever. The 'long term' never seems to have arrived.

The problem isn't technology. It's politics.

The public remains firmly opposed. Infamously, a petition attacking New Labour's investigations of the scheme was so popular that it crashed the Number 10 website. It went on to attract nearly two million signatures. No tax rise is popular, but that doesn't explain the scale of antagonism to nothing more a proposal.

More broadly, a survey for MORI suggested that 48 per cent of the public are opposed to road charging, with 29 per cent of these strongly opposed. In comparison just 33 per cent are in favour.[164]

So, why this popular hostility to a policy so beloved of policy wonks?

The best answer is that drivers no longer trust the government.

And Why Would They?

Taxes on drivers continue to rise, but the government refuses to build more roads. In 2006/7 for example, the Treasury took in £28bn in tax revenue from the roads – and in return spent less than half that at £12.77bn. At the same time urbanist Planners are forever claiming that we should move away from cars altogether.

Yes, cars have their problems. It is important to put in place effective safety controls, and to investigate new green technologies such as hybrids and electric cars. It is right that drivers pay some excess taxes to compensate society for the costs these externalities impose.

But the current tax surplus already more than covers these externalities. Many safety regulations seem to be

---

164 Support For Road Pricing If Revenues Used For Public Transport, 22 October 2007, Ipsos Mori

making little difference to health other than creating hassle and irritation for ordinary drivers.

To some Planners, the purpose of road pricing or carbon taxes is not to make our transport or environment run better and more smoothly. It is to increase gradually the price of driving, making it unaffordable for the average person and forcing people to take the buses and trains that they have previously neglected to use.

It is no surprise then that advocates of road pricing have a serious PR challenge to raise support for their favoured policy. Let's look at some of the ways they could try to gain back public support.

One suggestion is that it would be easier to win support if the revenues were allocated exclusively for investing in public transport. Surveys have indicated that support rises to 61 per cent in this case.[165]

But there are other reasons not to go down this route. Such a move would struggle to be credible – initial road taxes were likewise promised to be ring-fenced for the roads, before rapidly being absorbed into the general public purse. Moreover, such a move would give credence to the idea that we are introducing road pricing in order to force people onto public transport.

That simply isn't the case. Road pricing is designed to make the roads work better, not to push people away from them. Initially the revenue from any road pricing scheme should be used by the Exchequer wherever it is most needed, but in the long run it makes sense to use it as a funding source for new investments in roads themselves. If a new restaurant is oversubscribed, then it should use its profits to expand, not subsidise a losing competitor.

A better suggestion on revenue is to bundle together any introduction of a road pricing system with the abolition

---

165   Support For Road Pricing If Revenues Used For Public Transport, 22 October 2007, Ipso Mori

of Vehicle Exercise Duty. The message should be the new system won't cost the average family any more than today's taxes. Indeed, it may save them money.

Polls give tentative support to such a move. Just under half of the public (49 per cent) would support road charging if the tax on petrol is reduced, while just over half would support this move if it were combined with lower road tax (53 per cent).

Aside from costs, a second often mentioned concern are the implications for civil liberties. Many seemingly natural political supporters of a road tax remain opposed, believing that its introduction would create a Big Brother state, allowing the government to track or even limit the movements of any car.

Although important, this objection is perhaps overstated. Any system will require strong technological safeguards to protect privacy, but we already live in an era where governments and private companies store vast amounts of data about us. Your mobile phone company already knows everywhere you've travelled, while Facebook can list your best friends. If today the government wants to track you, it already has many options through its CCTV network and abilities to scan our emails.

Ultimately, this is a problem of implementation rather than a fundamental objection, and other issues will similarly need to be debated. Should the entire country convert at the same time to a nation-wide road pricing system, or should we instead focus on creating pricing zones for the most congested motorways and city centres on the model of London's Congestion Charge? Alternatively, should prices vary by road and time of day, or should we try to create a more stable pricing structure to give consumers predictability?

Such debates can continue. The direction of the reform is more important than the exact details of its initial incarnation.

Opening up the roads to private investors and creating a road pricing system are two sides of the same coin. Both measures take a system that has for too long been controlled by static government plans, and convert the road network into a far more dynamic entity, responding to the changing needs and requirements of customers. Ultimately, until such a market exists we will always face the threat of gridlock.

Such a reform is difficult, and would take a generation to put in place. We will not reform 'road socialism' easily. But we will not even be able to start putting its foundations in place, until we get over today's damaging feud between drivers and the Planners.

Cars are not going anywhere. They will remain part of the transport mix, now and for the foreseeable future. Driving is not evil, and has been the freely chosen choice of most families over the last century.

Until we end this 'war', we will never be able to persuade drivers that new ideas such as road pricing only have their best interests at heart. The Rebecca Rioters may have been one of the first groups to protest against road taxes, but they certainly were not the last. Until the government can persuade drivers that it really is on their side, it will simply be unable to be implement the reforms that our roads really need.

RAIL

In the early 1990s the Major administration decided to begin the process of returning the railways to private ownership. After all, the privatisation of the utilities, telecoms and aviation sectors had been successes for the last Thatcher government. In the US, the liberalising Staggers Act had increased the productivity levels of rail freight by 172 per cent, while rates halved.[166] There seemed no reason that British rail should not see similar gains.

The early plans of the reformers were, indeed, ambitious. By introducing as much competition within the industry as possible, reformers believed that they could use the power of market to boost innovation and cut costs. The monolithic British Rail was to be broken up into over two hundred new organisations. The core functions of building new stock, running the services themselves and maintaining the rail infrastructure were split into entirely new markets.

Twenty years later, the privatisation of the railways hardly seems an unqualified success.

In the end flexibility has practically vanished, as ever greater levels of targets and control of the timetable have been passed to the Department for Transport. A series of franchises and the track operator Railtrack have failed, or had to be bailed out by the government. The promised new competition from open access operators, in which any company could operate a competing service, never really took off. Maintenance has been taken back completely by Network Rail, and the industry as a whole suffered frequent safety scares. A constant stream

of government agencies were created and then taken
apart, ultimately resulting in the Department taking ever
more control.

Even worse than the increase in government control has
been the increase in government spending.

The spectacle of passengers complaining about ticket
rises has become an annual news ritual, but rising ticket
prices are only one of the ways the railways pays for its
addiction to new spending. Since its creation, Network
Rail's debt has risen from £9bn at its inception in 2002 to
£20bn in 2011. It is projected to be £31.5bn by the end of
2014, and the track provider will soon have to pay £1.7bn
every single year in interest on its debt.[167]

Even on top of this, the industry depends on the taxpayer
to survive. Around half of Network Rail's income and a
quarter of that of the train operating companies comes from
the taxpayer in the form of a direct subsidy. Government
subsidy to the rail industry as a whole is now over £5bn a
year. This is more subsidy than the government paid to the
industry even when it existed as a nationalised entity.

The message of this book has been that transport needs
less planning and more markets. Here clearly is an example
where our prescription has been followed – and yet seems
to have failed, or at best be severely disappointing.

Does the failure of privatisation discredit the whole idea
of markets in transport? And what exactly did go wrong
with the reformers initial plans?

What Went Wrong with Privatisation?
Out in the wilds of the free economy, market structures
evolve. Trying to create one on the blackboard of a
Westminster office is a more difficult task than is sometimes
appreciated.

---

167 http://www.christianwolmar.co.uk/2008/12/rail-607-trusting-
network-rail-is-hard-to-do/

The problem is that markets aren't planned – they grow.

There are two fundamental difficulties that face anyone who does try to plan a market.

The first is that any industry is a mix of two different forms of organisation: central command and control, and market competition. Sometimes a company will buy in its catering from an outside organisation, sometimes it will decide it is easier in-house. Industries evolve into complex webs of organisations, some supplying each other through bureaucratic internal chains of command, others through the pricing mechanism. Groupings evolve as firms acquire each other in mergers, or decide on outsourcing to save costs.

Every market planner then has to decide which functions should be linked together, and which functions should be broken apart. Should the company who runs the airline also own the airport? Should a train company own its tracks or trains? Should maintenance on the rails be done in house to ensure safety, or is it best to lease it out?

And then there is the other crucial aspect to evolution: the death of the ineffective.

Ambitious reformers often believe that all that is needed is a dose of bracing private sector managerial talent to pull a struggling public service body together, and increase its efficiency and productivity to commercial levels.

But there is nothing magic about the private sector. The idea that the private and public sectors each have their own ethos is somewhat overstated. Large private sector companies can just be as bureaucratic, stagnant and slow to act as any government body. This is part of the reason why most big companies eventually fail, unable to cope with changing market conditions.

The reason organisations in the private sector tend empirically to show higher levels of productivity is not that every organisation is equally brilliant, but that those that are ineffectual are allowed to fail. It is evolution, in its highly competitive selection process, that gives the private sector its efficiency.

When a market planner gets these questions wrong, we end up with the sort of problems we saw in the railway privatisation.

The government at the time believed that the industry would be improved by two complementary forms of competition. Firms would first compete to win the franchise contract to run the majority of trains in a region, and then they would compete again against small independent open access operators that would also be allowed onto the tracks.

It was soon discovered that trying to do both at the same time simply wasn't possible. The economics of the railway network dictate that the vast majority of routes will be loss making on their own, cross subsidised by the highly profitable few. It has been estimated that just 3 per cent of stations are responsible for 50 per cent of passengers.[168] Companies wish to gain a franchise which gives a local monopoly over part of the network, because of its expected revenue. If open access operators can take customers on their most profitable journeys, then companies will either not bid for the less successful franchises or require far more subsidy in the first place.

Even the greatest defender of the private sector would have to acknowledge that the early experiences of the franchises themselves have been disappointing. Many railway companies discovered that they had radically underestimated costs, and were forced to leave their contracts half way, or simply demand more subsidy. Gradually the government came to the view that they had to provide the franchisees with a greater security of revenue. The outcome

---

168 Leunig, Tim, 'What To Do About Trains in Britain', Policy Exchange, London, 2010, p. 9

of this greater subsidy was that the government wanted greater control.

The original intention of the reforms was to reduce government subsidy and intervention, but in practice the exact opposite seems to have occurred. As we saw earlier in Chapter 6, eliminating government owner-ship by itself is not enough to do away with government control. Policy tools like subsidies, price regulation and the Regulatory Asset Base give the Department of Transport as much or more control than it ever had in the days of British Rail.

The experience of privatisation does not show that markets don't work in transport. But it does show that returning an industry to private control is far harder than simply leaving it alone in the first place. Governments have far less ability to create new, healthy markets than they like to believe.

Why do the Railways Cost so Much?

While spending on roads is cut and aviation constrained, investment today in the railways continues to thrive. Even putting to one side High Speed Rail, the present govern-ment seems to be planning a never ending list of new invest-ments. There will be new urban links such as CrossRail and ThamesLink. The network will be refreshed with new train stock from the Intercity Express Programme. Huge new sections of the railway are to be electrified, allowing faster and greener services. The coalition government's austerity programme seems to be biting everywhere but the railways.

Many grand hopes are laid on the railways. After a long stagnation in the post-war period, passenger numbers are once again on the rise. They are seen as the environmentally sound alternative to the dirty technologies of car and aero-planes. New stations and tracks are seen as crucial tools of economic redevelopment, and the proposed High Speed

2 line is viewed as a useful measure to bridge the North–South divide.

British voters seem almost as sentimental about the railways as their politicians, the legacy of the old train spotters still remains. Strong passions are enflamed in the defence of local railway services. New developments are nodded through in a way that is simply unimaginable for other modes of transport. While the new High Speed 2 line has faced some backlash, it isn't hard to imagine the reaction if the government had announced the construction of a major new motorway network instead.

The increasing importance and scale of the railways makes it more important to understand what we can do to make them more efficient, and finally do away with the growing fares, subsidies and debt.

There are many suspects for the rise in the railway's costs, but perhaps the most oft repeated theory is the break up between track and wheel.

The idea is simple. Ever since the very first railways were opened in the 1820s, railway companies have largely chosen to own both the track and the trains that run on it. While this means careful deals for access have to be made with freight trains and other intercity services, this has been found overall to keep down costs.

There are simply too many interactions between the trains and tracks to break apart their functions into separate organisations. The heavier the train, the more maintenance the track will need, while the facilities any train operator can run depends on the track.

When these functions aren't combined in the same body, the companies instead have to enter into extensive negotiations over who is responsible for what. While this is a boon for bureaucracy and lawyers, it slows down decision making and makes it harder to implement reforms.

The thesis that breaking up track and wheel has been disastrous for containing costs is persuasively put forward by left leaning commentators such as Christian Wolmar,[169] but also less likely bodies such as the Institute for Economic Affairs[170] and even the Libertarian Alliance.[171]

In general, it is argued, fragmentation of the railways into many different companies reduces economies of scale and increases costs. Some even argue that it puts in danger safety measures, and that accidents such as Hatfield would not have happened if Railtrack hadn't outsourced its maintenance work.

However, while fragmentation certainly hasn't helped in many cases, it seems unlikely to be the sole culprit for the cost increases. After all, the separation of vehicle and infrastructure works well enough in the road and air markets.

Another factor that is worth considering is the costs of increased safety measures.

In retrospect the worries about safety seem exaggerated by media images ready for the evening news. Rail remains a much safer mode of transport than the roads. The cost of the safety measures introduced by the rail industry was vastly out of proportion to measures in other industries. In any case, research by Professor Andrew Evans[172] shows that safety under the privatised companies was improving, and showed no deterioration from the days of British Rail. A few emotive incidents obscured this trend.

But if the benefits of increased safety procedures were largely illusory, the costs were all too real. In the short term the aftermath of the Hatfield rail crash was to prove fatal to Railtrack. Panicking that the broken rail responsible for the

---

169 Wolmar, *On the Wrong Line: How Ideology and Incompetence Wrecked Britain's Railways*, 2005

170 'The Railways, the Market and the Government', Institute for Economic Affairs, London, 2006

171 Crozier, 2001

172 Evans, Andrew W., 'Rail safety and rail privatisation in Britain', Imperial College London, 2004

accident could just be the first lurking in the wider network, Railtrack implemented extensive speed restrictions and urgent maintenance work all over the network. This was prohibitively expensive, and Railtrack soon lost the confidence of its investors. The Labour government was only too happy to let it slide into administration, and then in effect renationalised it by creating the government backed non profit Network Rail.

More invidiously the concerns over safety have acted as a permanent source of pressure pushing prices up and contributing to the loss of fiscal discipline. It was only too easy to argue that more and more investment was needed to ensure safety. Investors were only too happy to provide this investment, swapping their capital for government-backed loans. The railways fitted in with the mood of the times. They were simply yet another public service that needed funds to compensate for decades of underinvestment.

The British railways are clearly now inefficient. Figures by the Office of Rail Regulation suggests that Network Rail remains 30 to 50 per cent less efficient than other European railways. In general, civil engineering costs in the UK are double those in Europe.[173]

This doesn't seem to be an inevitable result of privatisation. Other regulated sectors have seen their costs drop by 4 to 6 per cent a year. In Europe, the introduction of franchising in Germany and Sweden created cost reductions of between 20 to 40 per cent. By contrast, the costs of both Network Rail and the train franchises remain above their level in 1996.[174]

So, Why Have the Costs Increased?
Unfortunately, there is no simple single answer.

---

173   Rail Value for Money: Scoping Study Report, 2010, p. 7
174   Ibid.

The most benign cause is that since privatisation the railways have seen large increases both in the passengers carried and freight moved. The railways now carry 95 per cent more passengers, 1.3bn per year in total, and 37 per cent more freight.[175]

At the same time, standards have improved to some extent. Aside from the safety improvements, there have been upgrades in reliability, capacity and even customer satisfaction.[176] The railway has seen significant new enhancements, such as the West Coast Main Line upgrade and the opening of the High Speed 1 line.

But unfortunately these improvements aren't enough to explain the increase in costs. No part of the railways seems entirely immune from the inefficiencies.

The train franchises make up about a third of the railway's costs, at around £4.2bn in total.[177] That's an increase of about £1.4bn since privatisation. Around £0.6bn of this, or 40 per cent, seems to come just from the fact that the trains are now travelling further and serving more passengers. The rest seems largely to have gone on staff.[178]

Network Rail, by contrast, has total costs of around £6.0bn.[179] Its largest cost increases have come from major new projects such as the West Coast Main Line and Thameslink (around £1.1bn) and the renewal and repair of track (around £2bn).[180] These costs peaked in the wake of the Hatfield rail accident, but although they are on their way down they are still far higher than those in its European counterparts. A report by the Office of Rail Regulation tried to break down why these inefficien-

---

175   (Rail Value for Money: Scoping Study Report, 2010), p. 13
176   Ibid.
177   Ibid., p. 15
178   Ibid., p. 16
179   Ibid., p. 15
180   Ibid., p. 17

cies existed. It concluded that although a large part of the cost difference was poorly understood, among the many reasons were less effective contracting strategies for outsourcing, the particular circumstances of the British network and inefficient methods of taking over the track for maintenance work.[181]

In short, we are investing far more in the railways. We have increased the number of staff. We have tried to reform the system, while not overtly affecting ongoing performance, with mixed results.

The record of the railways sounds much like any other public sector in the New Labour era. Vast amounts of money invested, but very little of sense of what return is being gained for the additional cash.

We may never know for sure the exact reasons why costs have ballooned in the railways. What we do know is that the current structure isn't working.

Who is in Control?

Over the last twenty years, control of the railways has gradually been centralised away from the customers and day-to-day workers, and placed in the hands of an almost all-powerful Department for Transport.

It is the Department that sets the train timetables and decides what services are to be offered. It is the Department which determines what major strategic track upgrades to undertake, such as electrification or new high speed networks. It is the Department that decides when and what type of new stock to order. It is the Department who sets what prices will be on a good proportion of fares, the so-called regulated 'tickets'. And it is even the Department who decides what profits train companies should make, and how much they should be subsidised in turn.

---

181   International cost efficiency benchmarking of Network Rail, 2010

By setting out such detailed instructions, the franchise agreements make it harder for the train companies to try out new ideas or adapt to changing circumstances. When the unexpected occurs – perhaps a volcanic ash cloud stopping passengers wanting to travel to the airport, or even just the annual slow periods over Christmas – companies find it hard to adjust their schedules accordingly. Sometimes, the level of detail gets utterly ridiculous, as in the recent South West Trains franchise that specified the exact location of a vending machine at Wimbledon station.[182]

The Department's control is in turn filtered through Network Rail, the non profit body set up by the New Labour government to manage station and track infrastructure.

In theory, train companies such as First Great Western or Virgin receive their revenues from the tickets they sell to passengers. This money is in turn used to pay Network Rail for the costs of maintaining and operating the track. Control in this model passes up from customers to the railway companies and in turn to their own suppliers. This is how markets are supposed to work, the economic structure balanced on meeting the needs and requirements of customers. The consumer is in control.

But in reality, control flows in precisely the opposite direction. First, government decides what services it wants to offer. Accordingly, it then allocates subsidies. Some of this subsidy goes directly to the companies operating the trains, but most goes to Network Rail. This allows Network Rail to hold down the prices it charges the railway companies for using the track, far below its actual costs.

The implication of this complicated funding structure is that the best way for any railway company to make profits is to keep the government happy, rather than worry about the customer. It is the government who decides what services you are going to offer, and how much profit you are allowed to make. It is government who has control of the crucial subsidy system.

Who in this System is in Control of Keeping Costs Down?

The funding requirement for Network Rail is now decided by the independent regulator, the Office for Rail Regulation, so the Treasury can no longer keep such a tight eye on the railway's costs. Network Rail itself can raise as much money as it needs through the Regulatory Asset Base model. In any case, as a non profit organisation, it has no real incentive to cut costs. The train companies in turn have their profits controlled by government regulation. Cutting costs will just mean that they receive fewer subsidies.

Fixing the Railways

If we are ever to bring the bill for the railways back in control, then we will need to put the individual customers back in charge. But to do that will require fundamental reform at every level.

First of all, we will have to clear up the confusing flows of money through the system. The easiest way to do that is to make sure that Network Rail exists to serve the railway companies, rather than the other way around. Rather than subsidise Network Rail who then in turn subsidise the railway companies, we should cut out the middle man and give the money directly to the railway companies. This would give us a much better idea of how much operating the tracks actually costs.

Then we'll have to reform the current system of franchising, giving railway companies far more freedom and flexibility to make their own decisions. There is no need for the Department of Transport to micromanage the location of every vending machine. At the same time we will have to put in place in better facilities for what to do when railway franchises fail. Our goal should be to make sure that when any company fails they can neither hold the government to ransom nor shut down the railway network. We cannot ensure that every company who enters the industry should be guaranteed a profit.

Of course, while these reforms are still probably necessary, they are far from sufficient. On their own they would do little other than recreate the original structure that was imposed in the original privatisation in the early 1990s. Although there were clearly ideological reasons for the New Labour administration's move away from this system, it would be naive to believe that the last administration's drive for greater central control was *solely* driven by ideology.

Creating more flexible franchises on its own is not enough. It needs to come as part of a package deal alongside two other crucial reforms.

Network Rail is currently internally divided into seventeen different routes, each with their own utilisation strategies. There is however a growing agreement that Network Rail needs to be restructured into a far more regional structure. This seems to be the view of Philip Hammond, the Secretary of State for Transport in 2011. This is favoured by the TOCs and their industry organisation ATOC, and is supported by the ongoing recent report into value for money. Sensing this agreement, the new CEO of Network Rail David Higgins announced, within his first few weeks on the job in early 2011, a plan to devolve power to nine new regional organisations. The real debate seems to be no longer about whether decentralisation should take place, but to what extent each region should be given autonomy.

One possibility would be to separate the company into new regional components, ideally in a geographical manner to match the current franchise areas.

The first and most immediate benefit of this change

is that it would give us far more information. At the
moment, decisions on subsidy and regulated prices are
based on Network Rail's own information and cross country comparisons. While helpful, these are never perfect
analogues of the British situation. A regional model by
contrast allows the regulator to compare each firm against
the other. We already use a similar model in the water
industry where it has worked well. Costs for the privatised
companies are far below the still nationalised industry in
Northern Ireland.

But there are other benefits as well. If we have learnt one
lesson from privatisation, it is the difficulties in trying to
plan the perfect structure for a market ahead of time. When
our railways no longer act as a single national network, we
can make far greater use of experimentation to see what
works and what doesn't.

We should actively encourage different regions to
experiment with different models. When we are looking to
reform the entire railway network at once we must necessarily be cautious, but in changing one region we can be
significantly bolder. Neither is there any need for a 'one size
fits all' strategy.

Suppose we believe that the real problem with privatisation was the division of track and wheel. Under our
new regional system, we could look into merging some
railway franchises and the new infrastructure providers.
On the other hand, in other areas we could look into the
opposite approach, and attempt to introduce more open
access operators to create as much on-track competition
as possible.

Perhaps more controversially, at some point we could
look again into the privatisation of some of these new
regional infrastructure operators.

While reining in costs has to be the priority, a return of
shareholder equity and a more private sector ethos might
help with the other side of the equation: increasing revenue.

Politicians such as John Redwood[183] have complained that Network Rail has shown little innovation or initiative to take advantage of commercial opportunities. Train stations usually own highly valuable land in the middle of town centres, complete with captive customers looking for nourishment and entertainment. It is notable that airports have succeeded so well in providing retail opportunities that they earn as much revenue from shops as planes.

Indeed, if the timelines were co-ordinated the bidding process for train and track franchises could be aligned, allowing companies to decide for themselves whether they wish to bid for both.

Fixing the Politics

While these changes could help to make the railways more efficient, they will not be sufficient in themselves. Costs will almost inevitably continue to rise without limit while there remains a never ending government subsidy. To fix the economics of the railways, we must at the same time fix the politics.

Just as in planning, the benefits of any line are concentrated while its costs are diffuse, giving disproportionate power to special interests and lobbyists. The result is a network still largely optimised for Victorian needs. At the same time, subsidy continues to rise and central government itself faces huge incentives to become more involved in the day to day running of the railways.

The best solution would be to devolve budgets, responsibilities and decisions to local communities. It is much harder to accept far off decisions given by distant bureaucrats than hard choices agonised over in the local press. As we have seen in recent public debate, the public is prepared

---

183 Redwood, John, 'Can anyone make the train take the strain?', London, 2008, http://www.johnredwoodsdiary.com/2008/01/30/can-anyone-make-the-train-take-the-strain/

to accept hard decisions in the face of economic austerity, but only if it believes a fair process has been followed. At the same time, we cannot expect the national press to be concerned about the fate of every small railway line.

Rather than drawing from an unlimited pot of government money, we should force communities to face the necessary difficult decisions. A community could choose to invest heavily in its local railway, or alternatively it could prioritise investment in local schools and hospitals.

Aside from introducing a measure of fiscal discipline into the debate, a further benefit of this reform would be that it would change the incentives of the companies in the railways. No longer would they solely be focused on government and the regulator; instead, they would have to impress their own local customers. This can only be helpful.

Simply on their economic fundamentals, we would not expect the railways to be a particularly efficient industry. None of the companies involved face much if any competition. Large parts of the network are run only because of government subsidy. Ticket payers are significantly subsidised by tax payers, helping demand to grow. The government has to intervene continuously by giving subsidies.

One way to think about the UK railways is to draw the analogy to the US healthcare system. In both, we have a complicated mix of private and public funding. In both, an excess of bureaucracy, administration and paperwork has helped inflate costs considerably. In both, there is little incentive to keep demand down, as customers do not face the full costs of their actions. Understandable concerns about life, death and safety have pushed costs beyond the point that is reasonable.

The recipe for reform in rail is likewise not too far from the usual objectives of healthcare reform. Customers must take more responsibility for their own costs, rather than be subsidised by the taxpayer. Government needs to set strategic objectives, but then leave implementation to those closer to the front line. The providers in the industry need to be broken up to allow more experimentation, democratic accountability and, whenever possible, competition.

The government is currently investing large amounts of money in the railways. If we have learnt anything from the New Labour era it is that rapid expansion of funds is no real substitute for reform.

AIR

It is a time of expansion in aviation. Across the globe, cities with global aspirations are constructing new gleaming terminals of steel and glass.

None have more ambitious plans than Dubai. Already vast in scope – its Terminal Three is the largest building in the world by floor space,[184] consisting of 1,185,000 m² in floor, the equivalent of 170 football fields – the city remains unsatisfied.

A new facility is being constructed, the Al Maktoum International airport, ten times as big again as the current Dubai International Airport and Dubai Cargo village combined. Its five runways will allow up to four aircraft to land simultaneously, twenty-four hours a day. All this is on top of the two runways at the already existing Dubai Airport, the two linked together by high speed railway. At the same time, the builders are constructing the largest parking facility in the world to contain its workers and guests, including spaces for up to 100,000 cars.

But then, Dubai has to make sure it can compete with the rest of the world where airports are everywhere growing rapidly in scale. The world's biggest airport, Atlanta, already has five runways. The second and third biggest, Chicago O'Hara and Dallas Forth Worth, have seven each. Amsterdam Schiphol has six, Paris Charles de Gaulle and Tokyo have four, Beijing and Frankfurt three (and one more under construction).

---

184   http://www.dubaiairport.com/DubaiAirports/English/
      Media+Center/Fact+Sheets/T3+Sept+Final.htm

Dubai's two current runways will clearly not be enough, if it is to get the real prize.

Ever since the deregulation of the 1980s, aviation has increasingly depended on a hub-and-spoke model. Rather than fly directly between two disparate locations, customers first fly into a larger central hub airport which then connects to other airports. This allows passengers to access a greater variety of destinations more easily. A small airport such as Edinburgh can only ever offer a limited range of itineraries – connect into Heathrow first, and you can travel on into the world to wherever you wish.

A crucial question for forthcoming decades is what destination will become the primary hub for west Eurasia, securing a profitable future for its trade and airlines. Will it be one of the European airports, such as Charles de Gaulle or Schiphol, or will it be Dubai?

This is the prize Dubai seeks, to become the interconnection for the globe – and the largest airport in the world.

Welcome to Britain

Imagine a businessman arriving in Britain, at the end of a long day.

He has already been up for the best part of twenty-four hours, his body clock completely displaced by the unnaturally long light outside. His body aches, having spent much of that time crammed into a tiny seat, distracting himself by eating tasteless food and watching bad television.

His mood wasn't helped by the long time he had to wait as planes circled the airport, waiting for a landing slot, but at long last, he is here. Exhausted, he leaves the plane – and finds himself in the middle of a building site.

Grimacing, he walks along seemingly never-ending miles of corridors, trying to ignore the grimy state of the building. Outside, the sky is dark and grey.

The queue for security seems to take forever, but in the end it doesn't make much difference – he is waiting for the best part of an hour for his baggage to make its way to the carousel, the ground crew apparently short of staff due to a strike.

As he pushes his trolley through customs he notices a faded poster on the wall:

'Welcome to Britain.'

The Airport Experience

Of course, in many ways this story is an unfair caricature. Often everything goes smoothly, and the airport experience can be pleasurable.

But it's easy to bring to mind the usual complaints about airports. Do we really need the ever growing list of restrictions on what can be packed in hand luggage? Why do British airports seem rundown and in a poor state of repair? And do airports always have to build more duty-free shops rather than seats for customers?

Heathrow Airport, for example, seems a paradox: one of the busiest airports in the world and yet suffers a mixed reputation. Rarely a year seems to go by without a new scandal popping up: a light fall of snow leading to days-long disruption, the unfortunate opening of Terminal Five, new convoluted security arrangements.

Some of these problems are a result of age and a history of government underinvestment, but the largest limitations come simply from it being so busy. The airport feels crowded because it is crowded, as it attempts to survive in the premier league of world airports with only two runways. Things often go wrong, because without any space capacity, there is zero margin for error. Early problems reverberate throughout the rest of the day's schedule. Heathrow, an airport that was originally designed to cope with a maximum of 50 million passengers, now sees over 60 million pass through each year.[185] The recent opening of

---

185   Keith Boyfield, Plane Commonsense: The case for feeder-reliever airports in the South East, Adam Smith Institute, 1994, p. 8

Terminal five has helped, but the airport's runways still run at nearly 99 per cent capacity.[186]

When the last aviation white paper was published in 2003, the South East had around 120 million journeys each year, and each of Heathrow, Gatwick and Stansted were already at near full capacity. At the same time, it predicted demand in the order of 500 million passenger a year by 2030.[187] The white paper concluded that an additional three new runways were needed to meet future demand, and recommended immediately building a third runway at Heathrow and a second runway at Stansted. Ever since then, demand has continued to grow, if anything at a faster rate than predicted by the original estimates. There was only a slight temporary slowdown of 2 per cent in the economic recession of 2007–8.

Capacity constraints have already started to affect Heathrow among its European competitors. In the last twenty years, it has fallen from first to fifth in terms of destinations served, and has a much inferior service to its competitors for the growing BRIC (Brazil, Russia, India, China) economies.[188] While Heathrow contends with two runways, Amsterdam Schiphol has six, and both Charles de Gaulle near Paris and Madrid have four. Frankfurt currently only has three runways, but its owners Frapol are looking to build a new runway and terminal.

And yet, for all its problems, Heathrow is near full at all hours of the day while spare capacity exists at Gatwick and Stansted, especially at non peak hours.

Why don't airlines use the other airports more? And, if Heathrow is to be limited to two runways in the future, then how on earth will it compete with booming locations such as Dubai?

---

186   Economic Impact of Hub Airports, British Chambers of Commerce, July 2009
187   The Future of Air Transport White Paper, 2003
188   The Economic Impact of Hub Airports, 2009

Is There Any Alternative to Heathrow?

Is Heathrow a monopoly?

Certainly, BAA held a monopoly on London airports in the past. When its airports were privatised, the government joined them together under a simple company controlling Heathrow, Gatwick and Stansted. This it was believed was the simplest solution to unlock the needed private investment.

But, as is the case in most industry monopolies, this has never been entirely satisfactory. The suspicion has always been that BAA has favoured Heathrow for its investment, and let its attention on Gatwick and Stansted slip. Without any effective competition, there is always the risk that any monopolist will provide poor customer service and raise prices too high.

In order to prevent this, every five years the Civil Aviation Authority (CAA) sets out price limits for Heathrow, Gatwick, Stansted and Manchester airports. These limits, it is believed, ensure that the airport operators don't take advantage of their monopoly power to earn excess profits or reduce service quality.

The days where BAA owned all three airports are now over. In recent years the Competition Commission has investigated the company twice, believing that the single monopoly was harming customers' interests. First BAA was forced to sell Gatwick in October 2009 and in March 2011 the Commission confirmed that it must divest itself of Stansted as well. Already there are signs that the new owners of Gatwick, Global Infrastructure Partners, have made real improvements.

Nevertheless, the regulator CAA retains its control over Heathrow's prices – and the airlines welcome this.

They argue that Heathrow is still a monopoly.

Why?

The answer comes back to the idea of hub airports. Only Heathrow, it is argued, has the scale to act as an effective hub airport. This not only offers a far higher level of choice and frequency of service for the passenger, but also allows each particular route to be more profitable for the airline, earning them an extra 15 to 20 per cent per passenger.[189] The 1993 'Runway Capacity in the South East' report produced similar figures, suggesting it could be worth an extra £20 per passenger to the airlines. As profit margins are so tight, this can make the difference between whether a flight is profit or loss making.

Many flights at Heathrow simply would not be sustainable at Gatwick. Indeed British Airways' own attempts to create a second hub at Gatwick in the 1990s eventually had to be abandoned when they discovered it to be unprofitable. Main airlines argue that expansion of capacity anywhere but Heathrow is largely pointless.

However, we should not accept this argument uncritically. As we discussed in Chapter 6, the prices of slots at Heathrow have long been kept too low through badly designed price regulation. In the long term, the sustainable future for British aviation must compromise on both an increase in capacity and an increase in the price level of tickets from our busiest airports.

Similarly we have already seen that the threat from climate change is not in itself a reason to hold back growth of the sector. Aviation already pays a high level of tax through Air Passenger Duty. In 2006 this raised £961m, and a doubling of the rates in 2007 saw the total reach £1.8bn.[190] According to the Department for Transport itself this in effect means that aviation already pays £100m more than the costs of both its carbon emission and local pollution. In other words, consumers have made their choice – they are prepared to use their limited carbon ration on aviation.

There are other reasons to be in favour of an expansion of aviation. A thriving aviation sector is important

189 A Market in Airport Slots, Institute for Economic Affairs, London
190 Air passenger duty bulletin April 2008, HMRC

to our wider economy. According to the Department for Transport, aviation contributed 1.1 per cent of GDP in 2004 and employed 186,000 people. A further 520,000 jobs depend indirectly on aviation while visitors arriving by air contribute £12bn a year and a further 170,000 jobs.[191]

In the era of globalisation, trade and transport links have only become more important. We cannot expect to gain more trade with China if our businessmen do not have a regular service flying there. A recent report suggested that using the same methodology which showed a Net Present Value of £10bn for the High Speed 2 rail link would show a benefit of around £30bn for a third runway at Heathrow.[192]

Moreover, there is a real argument on grounds of greater social equality in favour of increased aviation capacity. Aviation has brought international travel, and what used to be the province of the aristocracy and super rich, to the middle classes, but still remains unequally distributed. The poorest are more likely to holiday by the beach, while the rich take in cruises, ski trips, trips to the summer house in France and so on. Over 50 per cent of those with incomes below £20,000 didn't fly at all in the past year, while over 50 per cent of those with incomes of £31,000 took two flights or more. To cut off aviation capacity at the current level would be merely to maintain it as the province of the rich.

Where Should We Build a New Runway?

The approach to Kai Tak in Hong Kong was the most famous in the world, adored by passengers and pilots alike. At just under 700 feet the pilot would have to pull the plane into a sharp right turn, descending through Kowloon's apartment blocks. Watching through their

---

191   The economic contribution of the aviation industry in the UK, Oxford Economic Forecasting 2006 http://www.oxfordeconomics. com/Free/pdfs/Aviation2006Final.pdf

192   The Economic Impact of Hub Airports, 2009

windows passengers could almost see right into the flats around them, while those on the roofs of the buildings watched planes shoot past at eye level.

However, while being located right in the midst of crowded Kowloon might have been convenient for catching a taxi on landing, it made expansion impossible. One of the world's busiest airports, by the early 1990s the airport had long exceeded its capacity requirements. One in three flights was experiencing delays. Flying at night was extremely difficult, due to the very large population nearby.

In 1990, as the ninety-nine-year lease on Hong Kong was running out, the British and Chinese governments negotiated a plan for a new two runway airport to replace the crowded Kai Tak by the time of the handover in 1997.

The $20bn plan is impossibly ambitious. In seven years, the engineers will have to design and build a new airport, a high speed rail line, two tunnels, a sixteen-mile highway, a bridge the height of a sixty-story building and the largest terminal in the world. Moreover, all this is to be built on land that doesn't currently exist, but will have to be reclaimed from the sea. The engineering challenges don't end there. The bridges have to be able to withstand Hong Kong's summer weather, which means an annual eight typhoons, each with winds over two hundred miles per hour. Furthermore they have to be built in such a manner that they make sure not to slow down any ships entering or leaving the world's busiest port. The rail system will have to go through five miles of tunnels. Meanwhile, the new roads are supposed to scale mountains so steep that current equipment simply can't climb them – in the end, the engineers realise it will be easier to simply expand Hong Kong by adding land to the perimeter of the island. All this must be done three to four times faster than the standard for a normal construction project. [193]

---

193   http://www.theatlasphere.com/columns/050520-perren-manrises.php

The project does not quite make its 1997 deadline, but it is finished one year later, and mildly under budget to boot. The last flight from Kai Tak, a Cathay Pacific, takes off on 6 July 1998 at 1:05. A fleet of trucks move over the last equipment and personnel. Seven hours later the new airport is open for business.

A decade later, and the airport continues to do well, although it too is becoming increasingly crowded. Already its officials are beginning plans to construct a third runway, and once more expand its capacity.

Meanwhile, in Britain, even amongst those who believe we need more airport capacity there is little consensus on where it should go.

The mainstream consensus, backed both by the aviation industry and the last New Labour government, is a marginal approach. This foresees creating one new runway each at Heathrow, Gatwick and Stansted. As this approach is flexible, the pace and extent of the work can vary with changing demand in the coming years. It utilises the already existing infrastructure and gains from the economies of scale that are already in place at airports such as Heathrow. The industry itself is confident that it could fund the work without any need for government subsidy.

But there are other serious problems with this proposal, the same issues that were eventually to see the third runway killed off by political protest.

Heathrow is alone among the major European airports in that its flight path crosses a significant portion of the city. This is a result of its orientation due west of London. All of London's principal airports have significant residential suburbs which suffer heavily from the noise and air pollution aeroplanes inevitably create. While the airlines are working on new technology to minimise these effects, any increase in capacity will inevitably cause more irritation to more people.

While most current estimates focus on the period up to 2030, there is no real reason to believe that aviation growth will just slow down after this point. While we may be able to fit one more runway at Heathrow and perhaps two at Gatwick, there is no practical means of ever being able to match Dubai's target of six. Even if we create three new runways official predictions suggest we might still require a further 540,000 slots by 2035/6,[194] the same capacity again as Heathrow today. In the long run, building on our current airport sites seems a dead end.

There is however another possibility. We could copy Hong Kong's lead. Rather than be constrained by the limitations of our current facilities, we could build an entirely new airport. Increasingly, proposals are being put forward for the creation of a new hub airport, most likely on purpose built islands in the Thames Estuary.

Such an airport could grow as large as is needed. It would avoid the current problems of local noise and pollution. It need require no Compulsory Purchase Orders or the demolition of historic churches or villages. The airport could finally operate a full twenty-four hours a day rather than be restricted at night, allowing both more freight and passenger flights.

The proposal isn't perfect. Strategically, a Thames airport would seem on the wrong side of London for the majority of the country, meaning that there is a strong case for continuing to run Heathrow and the airport at the same time. There are significant initial problems that would need to be overcome – but the example of Hong Kong shows that most things are possible with enough determination.

In any case, many of the supposed problems of the project are overstated. Critics complain about the dangers from a sunken Second World War munitions ship in the estuary or from the local bird population hitting approaching planes. While the so-called 'bird strike' will have to be carefully managed, this is a problem at all airports – in 2002

Heathrow suffered as many as seventy-one incidents of bird strike.[195] By building on artificial islands the airport can avoid the birds' current nesting grounds. If it is connected with the right high speed transport links it should be easily reachable from London, with journeys of under thirty minutes into St Pancras.

A crucial question is whether such a proposition is commercially viable. Current estimates suggest that the project should cost in the order of £40bn, a considerable sum. For comparison, Heathrow currently earns around £500m profit a year, and serves just under half of the current market. In other words, while in the very long term there is a good chance of the project making its money back, there is no guarantee. As we've frequently discussed in the past, such long-term projects are always to some extent based on guesswork.

There is however a not bad case for bringing in additional government funding to support the project. Independent estimates suggest that the project should generate around £20bn worth of value to the wider economy, and £10bn in productivity improvements. These numbers are of course guesses as well, but they present easily as strong a case for government investment as High Speed Rail.

A Thames Estuary Airport might not be the only solution to current capacity shortages, but we cannot continue to do nothing. The sooner we start seriously exploring options elsewhere, the less time we will have to put up with overcrowded airports. The Coalition's current 'better, not bigger' policy is difficult to envisage as a long-term solution.

The legacy of the South East's planning laws, government procrastination over long-term decisions, and a stagnant aviation monopoly have left the country with infrastructure that is inadequate. Capacity is already nearly full, while demand looks set to continue to grow. This is made worse by a poor regulatory structure, which encourages slots in Heathrow to be priced below market rates, and rations out demand by queuing rather than price.

The aviation industry itself has done a terrible job at defending its own interests. A coalition of local and climate campaigners has completely outflanked it, persuading the government to halt any increases in capacity. Meanwhile the industry has itself fixated on Heathrow as a solution, despite government warnings that the continuation of such a debate was futile. Both the government and the industry need to move on from the third runway debate.

Ultimately, Britain needs to make a choice. If it believes in playing a part in globalisation and in making sure travel isn't just the reserve of the rich, it will need more airports.

THE FUTURE

'**W**e'll probably put a first man in space in about three years,' claimed entrepreneur Elon Musk to the *Wall Street Journal Saturday* in early 2011. 'We're going all the way to Mars, I think... best case ten years, worst case fifteen to twenty years.'[196]

It is difficult to know which is more crazy: that entrepreneur Musk has an ambition to put a human colony on Mars, or that his CV so far suggests that he just might achieve it.

But then Musk has lived an extraordinary life.

Born in South Africa, he already had made his first $500 by the age of twelve from the creation of his own computer game. Unwilling to do military service in apartheid South Africa, at seventeen he ran away to Canada. Two BA degrees later in Economics and Physics, he had concluded that there were three important problems of the day: the Internet, clean energy and space.

The year was 1995, and as the internet bubble expanded Musk realised that it was now the time to dive into the first of his chosen tasks. He quit his graduate degree in Physics after just two days, and proceeded to build his first start-up, Zip2, a service that managed the publication of content for news organisations. By 1999, he had sold the service for over $300 million to AltaVista, and moved onto his next project, an online payment service company that was to become PayPal. That in turn was acquired by eBay in 2002, this time for $1.5 billion in stock.

---

196 http://www.physorg.com/news/2011-04-spacex-aims-mars-years.html

After his internet enterprise, he moved onto his two other chosen problems. He provided the funding and became chairman of his cousin's company SolarCity, a firm dedicated to the designing and installation of solar power systems.

He then joined and rapidly took over Tesla Motors, intending to deliver affordable electric vehicles to mass market consumers. Remembering his lessons in marketing from Silicon Valley, however, he first sought to target influential early adopters with the Tesla Roadster, a no-compromise electric sports car. Delivered in 2008, the car was the first fully electric vehicle capable of travelling on the highway, and arguably proved to be the spur that drove companies such as General Motors and the development of the Chevrolet Volt.

And then, of course, there was space. The most ambitious of all Musk's projects, part of his long-term vision of pushing humans out into space.

But then at the beginning of the millennium, the final frontier itself seems to be giving up the monopoly of state control. One of the most noticeable features of this new space race is just how much it is driven by the money and ethos of Silicon Valley. Spaceship One was funded by Microsoft money, while Google has put forward their own funds for the Google Lunar X prize, to be awarded to the first private team to land a robot on the moon. Quieter than the rest, Jeff Bezos of Amazon has launched his own suborbital space company, Blue Origin.

Musk rapidly realised that his mission to Mars would remain forever impractical while it cost so much to get craft into Earth's orbit in the first place. He refined his mission: to reduce significantly the $10,000 per pound it took to put a payload into orbit.

The only weapon Musk has in taking on the might of NASA, and the corporate giants Boeing and Lockheed that supply it, is relying on the same Silicon Valley techniques that gave him his first successes. In other words, keep teams as small as possible and eliminate all bureaucracy. He recruited the best, most experienced team he could find, and ensured that they would not spend their lives in endless meetings or working on designs that never left the drawing board.

Four years after the company was founded, it attempted the launch of its first Falcon 1 rocket. Thirty-six seconds after take-off a fire erupted from the engine, forcing it to crash. A year later, they tried again – the second rocket lasted five minutes. Another year, and flight three achieved an altitude of 200 km before a problem with its stage separation prevented it from going higher into orbit.

One month later, on 28 September 2008, they tried a fourth time – and this time it worked. It was the first successful launch of any privately funded liquid-propelled orbital launch vehicle. They had already obtained a contract with NASA to supply the International Space Station, and by 2009 the Falcon 1 was undertaking its first commercial mission, carrying a satellite into space.

The long delayed retirement of the Space Shuttle has arrived in 2011, while the International Space Station is expected to last until 2015. It is the Falcon 1's elder brother the Falcon 9 that will take the lead in transporting astronauts back and forth.[197]

For the next few years, the only manned rockets flying into space will be privately run.

The Importance of the Future

For fifty years transport technology has largely stood still. But just as new private companies are bringing much needed innovation to the space race, new entrepreneurs are also finally pushing ahead with new technologies on the ground as well.

---

197   Other missions will be run by the Cygnus, an unmanned vehicle created by Orbital Sciences Corporation and Thales Alenia Space.

As we will see, hard-working visionaries are building prototype cars that drive themselves, transit systems that offer the flexibility of cars, a vast array of new ways to move around our cities, and even holidays in space.

Is all this just science fiction, or pointless speculation?

It may seem odd speculating about technology that could still be decades from widespread adoption, but then transport has always required long lead times. At the moment, the country is busy debating the merits and flaws of a new High Speed Rail network, the shortest stretch of which won't open until at least 2025. If past precedent is any indication, the construction of a new airport would require at least two or three decades.

But by the time we reach 2040, let alone 2050, the new options we are able to purse may completely change the context of our decisions. Whether we like it or not, we are already making choices about projects and infrastructure that are expected to last for decades into the future. We can't make good predictions of this sort without considering the possibility that other variables may change. Tomorrow's world will not look like today.

More to the point, these new technologies create great possibilities for improving our quality of living and economy. Brad Templeton, an expert on self driving cars, argues that the technology has the potential, in the US alone, to save 35,000 lives, a million lives, around $230bn in accident costs and 50bn hours (or $1 trillion dollars worth) of people's time.[198] If we restrict ourselves to overly rigid plans, we risk crowding out the opportunities from new ideas.

It turns out that the greatest threat to new innovation may not be our own scientific shortcomings, but the rigidities brought on by the Planners.

As we will see, that would be a real tragedy.

---

198   http://www.templetons.com/brad/robocars/

The Car that Drives Itself

If you drove along the highway between Los Angeles and
San Francisco in 2010, you might have been fortunate
enough to see a silver Toyota Prius with a strange metallic
bar attached to its roof. This is one of the prototypes for
technology company Google's most ambitious experiment:
an attempt to re-engineer the way we drive.

The US Defense Advanced Research Projects Agency
(DARPA, for short) is known for its ambitious projects.
Famously, one of its earlier initiatives, ARPANET, was
an important predecessor to the Internet, while a list of
its current initiatives looks like something out of science
fiction. It includes battery powered exoskeletons for
the military, flying armoured cars and even DARPA
Silent Talk, an attempt to create computer powered
telepathy.

A driverless car, it theorises, would remove the necessity
for putting a soldier's life in danger in a war zone, and so in
2004 it launched a $1 million 'Grand Challenge', a compe-
tition seeking driverless cars that could drive a 150 mile
route through the Mojave Desert. More than 100 teams
initially registered for the challenge, and fifteen vehicles
entered the final race.

None of them finished. Carnegie Mellon University's
Red Team did best, and only achieved a rather uninspiring
seven miles.

Undeterred, DARPA ran the Challenge again in 2005.
Near 200 teams from across the world entered, and twenty-
three of these ran in the final race. Twenty-two of the
twenty-three beat the winner in 2004's performance, while
five vehicles successfully completed the entire course.

The winner was a car called Stanley. Interestingly, its
engineers soon realised that it would be impossible to write
software that could perfectly predict and plan the thousands
of different situations that drivers encounter. Instead, they
followed a more organic process of trial and error, taking

the car out and letting it log and learn from its mistakes. The car taught itself how to drive.

After the desert was conquered, DARPA moved onto the city. In 2007 they ran a third grand challenge, this time situated in an urban environment. While the course was shorter, at only sixty miles, the vehicles would have to obey traffic laws, and avoid and merge into other traffic, creating exponentially more difficult problems. Nevertheless, six teams still succeeded in finishing the course.

Some of the technological issues in creating a self driving car are relatively straightforward. Getting a car to operate its own steering, accelerator and brakes is relatively easy; many modern cars already operate completely 'by wire', meaning all the necessary hardware other than computers and sensors is in place. Similarly, navigation is a largely solved problem – many people already rely heavily on GPS to tell them where to drive.

Yet other issues are vastly more complex. Predicting the behaviour of other vehicles is difficult, but hardest of all is the avoidance of obstacles. Unless the vehicles are kept to their own secured environment, then the vehicles will necessarily have to deal with the unexpected. It is not an easy task for a computer to be able to work out what a human driver is about to do, to predict a child running after a ball in the street or to avoid a deer jumping out onto the road.

Then again, in just three years the technology progressed from struggling in a desert to confidently navigating an urban environment.

Google's own car represents the next generation, as its team was made up of many of the engineers who worked on Stanley and other DARPA Challenge vehicles.

Equipped with the latest in sensor technology and an extensive database of the roads they are navigating, the Google cars have confidently roamed in and around San Francisco, human engineers sitting in them only to take control in the case of an emergency. According to Google, the vehicles have already logged over 140,000 miles. The only incident was when a human driver crashed into the computer car as it waited for a red light.

The technology still needs development. It is nowhere near ready for widespread use, and the usual large drops in price of technology have not yet brought the cost of its advanced sensors into the reach of the average consumer.

Nevertheless, it is becoming increasingly obvious that the question is no longer if the technology will work, but when it will.

The Startling Implications from Self Driving Cars
So, if self driving cars aren't just science fiction, how big a deal will they be?

It is of course impossible to say, but experts suggest that their impact could be momentous. Their arrival would radically change many of the debates we have been addressing throughout this book.

The first benefit to a complete system of self driving cars is that they can travel much faster. There are several reasons for this. When the systems have been perfected, a computer has far quicker reaction times than a human. There is no risk that a computer will panic when something jumps in front of it – it should be able to accelerate or (more importantly) brake with greater efficiency and reliability. The safe speed limit for self driving cars, in particular on motorways, should be much higher.

Moreover, if every car is controlled by a computer, then the road system as a whole can move faster even in a congested rush hour. Computer cars can drive much closer together, optimising their speed to give the maximum through fare. Every extra human car added to the road imposes a fixed cost in the increased reaction times of the driver, slowing the whole road down until eventually the road disappears into gridlock. Computer cars don't face the same problem.

They're also likely to be much safer in most situations. There are currently around 1.2 million car crashes per year worldwide, causing around 50 million accidents.[199] Up to half of these accidents are caused by simple human error. A computer driver will never take its attention off the road, never fall asleep and drift into the next lane, never drink one too many at their local and swerve back and forth across the road. They have perfect 360 degree vision, with no blind spot. Through infrared and other technologies they can actually see much better at night or in foggy conditions than any human.

Some experts were initially worried that ordinary citizens would find it difficult to get used to the idea of self driving cars. After all, it takes a lot of faith when you're travelling at seventy miles per hour to put your life and that of your family completely in the hands of a computer. Just as the Victorians were initially worried about the dangers of the new high speeds achieved by steam trains, it may take a little time to become accustomed to this new technology.

Surprisingly, it turns out that this doesn't seem to be the case. In an intriguing experiment, scientists updated the mechanical Turk concept for the modern day. Instead of a fake chess playing machine, they gave their subjects a fake self driving car. Unbeknown to their test subjects, the car was in reality being driven by someone in the back seats, but to the passengers it seemed as if a computer was fully in control. Reviewed later, most passengers seemed to adapt quickly to this new technology, happy to read a newspaper and take their attention off the road. Fear of new technology doesn't seem to be a limiting factor.

It's a mistake to think that a world with self driving cars would be just like today but with much faster cars. The lesson of the past is that significant new modes of transport like the railways or the internal combustion provide not just a quantitative but qualitative difference as well. The

---

199   http://www.templetons.com/brad/robocars/numbers.html

railways were not just a faster stage wagon. New methods of transport change our society, the way we go about our daily routine and where we choose to live.

It's not difficult to think of the possibility of some new business models that would exist in a world of self driving cars. Hiring a taxi – in effect, renting a computer car – would become much cheaper, the human cost removed. Public transport would lose much of its appeal, even in busy city centres, as the relative costs of cars dropped. Ad hoc renting business models like Zipcar would become still more convenient.

They would give new mobility to the elderly, vulnerable and the young, who would no longer be restricted to their homes or waiting for the next bus. Many parents would be much happier if their children had a nice safe computer car to drive them home at the end of the night.

It's also thinking about the possibilities that open up when you no longer have to be in the car. Your car could drop you off in front of the airport, and then go off to park itself. For that matter, it could leave home an hour before your flight was due to land and come to pick you up. It could drive itself to a supermarket, where it could be loaded with your weekly shopping, and then return home all by itself. The difference between Tesco and Amazon would disappear.

This new world is likely closer than you might think. After all, aeroplanes already contain the ability to more or less fly themselves – even the ability to make a landing on their own. Cars already contain thousands of microchips to control internal processes and an increasing number of sensors to give them information about the outside world. The 2011 Chevy Volt, it is claimed, contains more lines of programming code than a F35 Strike Fighter.[200] Dedicated

---

200   http://www.wired.co.uk/magazine/archive/2011/02/features/ai-
       drivers-not-wanted

systems tend to be far more reliable than the eternally crashing computer operating systems that we're used to.

Even with no great single leap, the cumulative nature of progress is likely to mean that our cars become ever smarter, and take over more responsibility for our driving safety behind the scenes.

Self driven cars could make our roads faster, smoother flowing and safer. They would save millions of hours of our time, and create whole new business models. They could open up the possibilities for new types of urban vehicles and give mobility to the isolated and vulnerable. Used at their fullest extent, they could fully replace nearly all other urban transport methods. Perhaps this an overly optimistic vision, but even if they only achieve a limited fraction of this potential they will have a significant impact on our everyday lives.

Personal Rapid Transit

Imagine a world in which when you walked to down to your nearest tube station, you would be presented with your own carriage, around the size of a bubble car. You would tell it the exact street you wanted to travel to in London, and it would zip off into the network, automatically changing across tube lines to take you the quickest route. It could dart down perhaps the Piccadilly Line, and then slide across onto the Central.

Whist self driven cars have been predicted for decades, almost as long foreseen has been the notion of personal rapid transit.

The idea is simple: to combine the merits of the automobile and the train. The vehicles run on dedicated guide ways, and thus can take advantage of all its merits with regard to speed, safety and energy efficiency. However, at the same time they would also have all the merits of personal transport: choice, convenience and running when the user wants to travel, not constrained to some timetable.

Computer control drives the vehicles, allowing the routing of the vehicles to be flexible. The user can choose the exact destination that they wish to reach, rather than being carried along a single line.

Indeed, some technologists go even further than this. Why stop at the equivalent of a tube network? Why not have a complete network of rails going up to every drive way, so that you would only have to step up out of your front door to board your own transit vehicle and get whisked away into the network. We could replace our old network of roads with a new network of rails instead.

Unlike the many problems thrown up by self driven cars, the technology required to achieve personal rapid transit is very straightforward, and could easily be built tomorrow with the right level of investment.

Indeed, the world's first personal rapid transit system was built as long ago as 1975 in the American university city of Morgantown. The relatively small system connects the three campuses of the university with the downtown, and currently serves around 16,000 passengers a day. While as a pilot project the system predictably considerably overran its initial budget, since the system started operating it seems to have run well and proved relatively cost efficient.

Thirty years later, others are beginning to follow Morgantown's example. Masdar City, Abu Dhabi's under-development planned zero carbon city, wishes to ban petrol powered cars from its streets. Instead, it will operate an extensive Personal Rapid Transit system to move people around, utilising up to eighty-three stations and a planned 2,500 vehicles.

A more surprising innovator is none other than Heathrow Airport. At the time of writing, the airport was in the last stages of testing a new Personal Rapid Transit system, connecting the car park with the new Terminal five.

If this proves to be a success, BAA claim that they plan to expand the network through the rest of the airport.

Personal Rapid Transit was widely seen as the future in the 1960s and 1970s, and the solution for putting in place transit networks into urban areas that didn't have the density to support a full underground transit system.

Ironically, it sometimes seems that the current two camps in transport – those in favour of the car, and those in favour of transit – have extended their war into the future. The former believe that the future of our transport will belong to self driven cars, while the latter argues for personal rapid transit.

There are two huge significant problems with the technology, although arguably neither are insurmountable.

The first is the sheer cost of putting the infrastructure in place necessary to make the technology practical. This is doubly true in cases where the infrastructure would have to be squeezed into already tightly crowded urban areas. This is one of the reasons that we are now seeing the possibility for new Personal Rapid Transit networks raised in completely new or underdeveloped cities. Clearly the ultimate dream of trying to connect every house into a transit system would be vastly expensive.

The second problem however is political: it is not easy for the central planners of a city to undertake such an expensive and risky experiment. The technology of self driving cars has the advantage that it can be built up in a cumulative fashion, society only gradually having to move away from manual vehicles. A Personal Rapid Transit system has to get past the roadblock that is government.

No transport method is perfect for each and every situation, but widespread operation of self driven cars would have many of the advantages of a personal rapid transit network. The advantage that the latter has is that the technology is already in place, but sadly it seems more likely that technology will progress than that bureaucracies will overcome their caution.

Tomorrow's Transport

While self driven cars and personal rapid transit are perhaps the 'big two', they are far from the only possibilities for ways we will move ourselves around in decades to come. We are so used to our current status quo of cars and trains that the sheer range of possibilities that remain unexplored can be overwhelming.

There are examples of more modest applications of technology allowing vehicles to drive themselves. One of the easier and more predictable next steps is the gradual adoption of this technology on our current rail-based systems of public transport.

New systems such as the Docklands Light Railway already run automatically, although each vehicle does contain a member of staff on board. The further adoption of such technology will theoretically allow all our tube and trains lines to be run automatically, or at least remotely. The problems in the implementation in this case are to do with cost and looking after customers rather than technology.

Removing the driver from trains could have important effects. For a start, it would allow trains to run much closer together, increasing capacity. It would limit the possibility of strikes, and allow the running of the infra-structure for longer hours. In the long run, it should drop prices drastically.

Another continuing innovation is the continuing development of electric cars.

The problem with the technology remains, as it has been since Victorian days, the battery technology. Huge sums of money are being piled into the further development of lithium batteries, but matching the performance and cost of petroleum is still an ongoing project.

There are two competing visions currently being pursued.

The first wishes to replace completely the performance and specifications of today's petrol cars, and believes that, with a large enough research programme and the construction of country-wide charging networks, this is an achievable goal. Charging remains one of the largest problems with electric cars – even if the capacity of petrol can be matched for the vast majority of situations there is simply no way to charge a battery as quickly as petrol can be poured into an engine.[201] Instead, developers are experimenting with the possibilities of interchangeable batteries, or the possibility instead of hydrogen powered batteries.

The second approach by contrast doesn't seek to replicate perfectly today's cars. It splits different uses into different functions. These engineers argue that the average car is vastly over engineered for the jobs it spends most of its time doing. Today's vehicles average nearly 4,000 lb, take up a footprint of 100 ft^2, have a range of over 300 miles, can go from 0 to sixty mph in less than ten seconds and reach speeds as high as 110 mph. This makes the cars twenty times heavier than the average driver, or fifteen times the footprint of an office chair. Most of the time our cars only travel no more than forty miles on our daily commute or to collect the shopping – and at speeds that are significantly below 110 mph.[202] Burdening our vehicles with these unnecessary specifications has left us a legacy of heavy engines and heavier vehicles that is hugely wasteful.

On this alternative approach, we should make use of lighter, small vehicles for our travel in the city, charging

---

201　Some technologists would dispute this point, and believe that in around ten years the rapid charging of batteries will be possible. The MIT Electric Vehicle team claim to already be able to charge batteries of the right scale in just seven minutes (see http://www.wfs.org/Jul-Aug2010/Chin.htm).

202　These statistics come from http://www.wfs.org/Jul-Aug2010/Chin.htm.

them each night in the same way we might now charge our
mobile phone. At the same time, when we want to travel
longer distances we could go back to petroleum or perhaps
hybrid vehicles.

One British start-up, Riversimple, is seeking to
completely redesign the car. Consisting of just eight staff
and a budget of £20 million, the company is creating an
open-source hydrogen powered car. By limiting the car's
top speed to fifty mph, using carbon-fibre bodywork and
keeping the car small, the company has drastically cut the
power the car needs, and thus the expense needed to build
it. Mercedes-Benz is currently exploring its own hydrogen
vehicles, powered by 100 kW cells that cost €1 million
each. By contrast Riversimple's fuel cell is just 6kW, and
thus should cost just $3,000–5,000.[203] The company plans
to release the CAD designs of the vehicle for anyone to
download and modify.

Other thinkers go even further in looking past the car.
Cars are a fundamentally space extravagant form of transport, which cause enormous congestion problems. Once
you have combined electric power with computer control,
it becomes much easier to fundamentally reinvent the sort
of vehicles we drive in urban areas.

The much hyped electronic personal transporter the
Segway has proved, it is probably fair to say, a flop. But
there is a reason it attracted the attention and initial admi-
ration of Steve Jobs and Jeff Bezos, the leaders of Apple
and Amazon. Infamously, Jobs's initial impression was
reported as being "If enough people see the machine, you
won't have to convince them to architect cities around it. It
will just happen.'[204] The entrepreneur who has had a large

---

203   http://www.wired.co.uk/magazine/archive/2010/10/features/
      change-driver?page=all
204   http://www.wired.co.uk/magazine/archive/2009/11/features/
      digital-cities-words-on-the-street

influence on our computer, music, film, publishing and phone industries may have simply been wrong about our transport infrastructure; alternatively, he may have simply been too optimistic in his time predictions. The Segway may not reshape our cities, but perhaps other vehicles will.

Many futurists are now designing a variety of smaller, lightweight vehicles – bigger than a bicycle, but smaller than a car – that can effectively transport one or two people across urban areas. Aside from being more environmentally friendly, these vehicles allow a much greater number of people to fit on our roads.

Advances will come about not just through the vehicles, but the underlying infrastructure of the city itself. We are already moving into the era of the 'smart city', and this trend will only accelerate in future years. Specialised networks will keep track of all the traffic moving through the city, dynamically rerouting vehicles to minimise congestion and avoid newly developing obstacles. The condition of the roads will constantly be monitored by the cameras on computer controlled cars, and constantly fed back into a central database (similar systems are already being developed to allow each train to monitor the condition of railways). Dynamic speed controls will constantly keep traffic moving at the optimal rate for fastest through fare.

While you may think that this vision of different vehicles for different purposes will prove impractically expensive for the ordinary family, these futurists predict that we'll be far more prepared to rent vehicles for short periods. Using an app on our smart phone, we'll choose the vehicle we want: a large car to transport the whole family, a small one-person transporter or even a bicycle on a sunny day. This might all seem far fetched, but then again we are already beginning to see the start of such systems: Zipcars, rentable by the hour through an iPhone app, or even of course the new system of Boris bikes, copied from the Parisian system of Vélib. While there is something to be said for ownership and families will probably always want to own their own car, the everyday experience of commuters in big cities such as London today shows ownership is not always necessary.

Even this doesn't represent the full range of ideas that are out there, seriously being discussed.

Some ideas are strange. The Shenzhen Hashi Future Parking Equipment Co. has announced the development of a straddling double decker bus, to be prototyped in Beijing over the next few years.[205] To make best use of road space, cars actually can continue to drive under the straddling bus as it moves. The bus itself can travel at sixty km/h, take up to 1,200 passengers and run on electric power. This apparently is a cheaper option than attempting to build a new underground railway system.

Other ideas are so advanced and expensive that they may take significantly longer to develop. You may have heard of maglev trains, a type of High Speed Train in which the train is levitated on magnetic fields. This allows speeds far in excess of the current technology, but is unfortunately so expensive that it is currently only used for dedicated short distance transit in airports. The most famous maglev train still running connects Shanghai Airport to the city, covering ninteen miles in just seven minutes. Oddly, in a continuance of British airports' seeming preference for ambitious transport technology, the very first commercial maglev system opened in Birmingham, although continual problems meant that it was shut in 1995.

The Shanghai maglev travels at a maximum of 268 mph, but this is only at the very lower bound of the technology's capability. One very farsighted idea proposed the idea of a dedicated maglev tunnel spanning the Atlantic.[206] This

205   http://www.chinahush.com/2010/07/31/straddling-bus-a-cheaper-
        greener-and-faster-alternative-to-commute/
206   http://www.popsci.com/scitech/article/2004-04/trans-
        atlantic-maglev

vacuum tunnel would be submerged a few hundred metres under the ocean's surface, and then anchored with cables to the seafloor. Trains would be able to reach a spectacular 4,000 mph through the tunnel, travel from New York to London in around one hour. The originator of this scheme, Ernst Frankel, a professor of ocean engineering at MIT, claims that from an engineering point of view 'there are no serious stumbling blocks'. On the other hand, cost estimates peg the total budget at several hundred billion dollars, making this a project perhaps for a richer age.

And then there are other projects which require next to no technology at all. As well as leading development in self driving cars, Google has also invested $1 million into the opposite end of the range, a project known as Schweeb. This is genuinely interesting – a pedal powered monorail in which riders cycle in small glass pods along an overhead track. The inventors argue that this track could be stretched out between close urban destinations, making a green, healthy means to travel. The lack of wind resistance or friction makes travelling very effective, allowing the speeds of a fast cyclist with no more energy than walking. In a world where concerns over dignity made it hard for the Segway to gain any ground, it seems unlikely that Schweeb will achieve much success, although it is probably worth Google's $1m gamble.

More down to earth, another much simpler possibility (if more expensive) is the extension of dedicated bus tracks. Buses are far cheaper than trains, and can very easily be scaled up and down as demand varies. Travelling on a dedicated bus lane makes the experience almost as smooth and fast as a train, while their ability to rejoin traffic at the end of the journey allows them to travel to a far greater range of destinations. Cambridge Council is currently finishing the conversion of an old closed railway into the world's longest busway, although the project is both running far over budget and behind schedule.

The X Prize

In the twentieth century, nothing seemed to represent the power and potential of the state more than the space race.

It was the state that provided initial funding, which supported scientists and later put in the large resources needed to push beyond the Earth's atmosphere. Communist and Capitalist, left and right, partisans of all ideologies seemed to agree that it was only the government that could conquer this vast wilderness.

After all, just getting into space represented the mother of all barrier-to-entry problems. The vast amount of energy required to defeat the Earth's gravitational field ensured that getting up into orbit required vast resources. And why go up there anyway? Technological optimists talked of the value that rested in the minerals buried in meteors or the potential of solar farms, but the simple fact that every kilo pushed out of the Earth's pull requires hundreds of thousands of dollars meant these dreams could never be economical.

It would have to be the state that took the lead, pursuing a different motive than profit.

Initially, this approach seemed to work wonders. Russian Communism proved that it was not so technologically backward that it could not launch a satellite or man into orbit. Not to be beaten, Kennedy announced the most ambitious government target of them all – to put a man on the moon before the decade was out.

But after the success of the Apollo missions, disappointment began to settle in. The new Shuttle programme never lived up to its goals of creating a reusable spacecraft and suffered horrific safety incidents. While the International Space Station may have proved a boon for Clinton's democracy, it seemed a dead end as far it as came to space exploration. Seeking to reignite earlier enthusiasm the Bush administration announced new targets for returning to the Moon and then onto Mars, but the projects fell so heavily behind in cost and practicality that on taking power the Obama administration rapidly cancelled them.

But despite NASA's slump, the last ten years have been one of the most exciting in space exploration since the 1960s themselves. A new wave of private space start-ups has emerged, and while their achievements presently come nowhere near those of NASA, they are moving at rapid speed. New companies such as Space-X, Virgin Galactic and Bigelow Airspace are changing the face of space travel.

It is difficult to say why this change is happening at this precise moment. Partly it may be that technology and computer aided design have reached the point where it has become easier than ever for small, dedicated teams to compete with the might of the large bureaucracies. Partly it may just be that the relative failures of NASA have spurred on others who believe that they can do better. Or perhaps the current advances are just the result of geeks who grew up watching *Star Trek* and enjoy spending the vast piles of cash they earned from the Internet revolution.

One of the first indicators of what was to come was the Ansari X-Prize.

The early days of aviation saw rapid technological progress as investors sought to increase the speed, scale and range of the aircraft present. One of the spurs to progress were prizes, such as the series offered by the *Daily Mail* and its proprietor Alfred Harmsworth. In 1906 they offered a £1,000 prize for the first aviator to cross the Channel and £10,000 for the first non-stop flight between London and Manchester. In response, the satirical magazine *Punch* decided to offer its own £10,000 prize for the first flight to Mars and back within a week. Despite the ridicule, both of Harmsworth prizes would be achieved within four years by the French.

The $25,000 American Orteig prize was offered to the first aviator to fly non-stop from New York to Paris. Initially created in 1919 by hotel owner Raymond Orteig, it wasn't until 1927 that Charles Lindberg finally achieved the task in his *Spirit of St. Lewis*. The competition offered by the prize didn't just capture public interest, it spurred on investment many times the bounty put forward by Orteig.

Inspired by this story, in 1996 Peter Diamandis launched the X Prize: a $10 million reward for the first non government organisation to get a reusable manned spacecraft into space twice within two weeks. In the end, over twenty-six teams entered the competition, and just as in the Orteig prize vastly more than $10 million was spent on development. Perhaps *Punch* had been more prescient than it realised.

There is more than one way to get into space. The simplest, most direct and most used means is through a rocket pushing straight up.

The problem with a rocket is its expense. Basic laws of physics put limits on the amounts of mass it can take, and make it very difficult to create the reusable vehicle that will be necessary to generate an industry. Each pound of weight the rocket has to carry requires huge amounts of fuel – which in itself is not so great a problem as the enormous structures that are required to hold the fuel.

Scientists and science fiction writers have often envisioned alternative means of getting to space. One popular variant is a space plane, an aircraft that travels so fast it can simply take off into space. Unfortunately, to escape the Earth such a vehicle would have to travel at Mach 25, a speed far beyond today's engineering. Other, even more extreme, options are suggested: a space gun, propelling vehicles out, or a space elevator, dragging vehicles up a cable attached to a satellite.

The winner of the X Prize only needed to reach suborbital heights, which allowed the eventual victor Scaled Composite to use their own innovative two-stage vehicle, led by engineer Burt Ruban and funded by Microsoft billionaire Paul Allen. The first stage is a large plane, *White Knight*, that carries the second craft *SpaceShipOne* up to a height of around fifteen km. From there, the *SpaceShipOne* detaches, launches its own rocket engine and eventually coasts to heights of around 100 km, just at the edge of space.

Rutan's team won the prize after their two successful flights on 29 September and 4 October 2004. Perhaps just as incredible as the technological innovation was the speed with which the technology was then commercialised.

Spotting an opportunity, entrepreneur Richard Branson contracted out Rutan's team to help him found Virgin Galactic, almost certain in 2012 or 2013 to become the world's first space tourism company. Already hundreds of passengers are signed up for their $200,000 ticket departing from Spaceport America in New Mexico on the new *White Knight II* and *SpaceShipTwo*.

Clearly, this is just the beginning of the development of the technology. Aviation and automobiles also began as the expensive playthings of the rich, before technology improved and costs dropped enough to make them a practical option for mass transport. While suborbital flight by itself will never allow you to reach the moon, it does allow the possibility of much faster travel across the Earth's surface. Virgin Galactic has already suggested that its *SpaceShipThree* should allow for a two-hour flight time between London and Sydney.

But putting aside such utilitarian considerations, it is worth considering the magnitude of what such companies as Virgin Galactic are suggesting.

If all goes to plan (and so far it has), costs will rapidly fall. Within your lifetime, you too will be able to travel to New Mexico, board a strange looking plane and blast off into Earth's atmosphere. You'll float in zero gravity, and stare down at the fragile, blue face of our planet.

That really is the future.

CONCLUSION

Gridlock Planet?

The long twentieth century experiment with state control of our transport seems to be coming to an end. Pricing is coming to our roads, train companies are being privatised, and airport monopolies broken up. Now, as we have seen, even space is one more sector in which the government monopoly has been broken apart.

In many ways the nation state is simply no longer big enough to manage transport. Global infrastructure corporations put in place roads and railways, protectionism is disappearing from the seas and the future of the air seems to be three grand global airline coalitions. In a globalised world, the links between our countries are as important as the links inside them.

Likewise, across the world we see the same furious arguments and debates. Is the future High Speed Rail, or is it more important to invest in extra road capacity? Can we afford to keep letting aviation expand unabated? Should we be trying to persuade drivers to use their cars less, and if so, how do we do it? How will we stop the megacities of the future from descending into gridlock?

There are three fundamental tasks that dominate the debate about the future of our transport systems, and – this book would argue – two possible answers.

The first problem is congestion. This problem has bedevilled us since Roman days, but it is only getting worse in an increasingly urbanised and crowded world. Unchecked, it threatens not only to clog up our roads and cause immense frustration, but halt the growth of the cities that will be at the heart of our future economy. We need to tackle and defeat this problem if we are to unlock future economic growth. If we are not careful, Beijing might not hold its record of a ten-day traffic jam for long.

The second problem is climate change. The Victorian transport revolution was founded upon harnessing the vast power of fossil fuels, but our planet can no longer afford their cost. The biggest battle in the war against global warming will be the generation of energy, but even if we solve this problem, on its own it will not be enough to tackle transport's own issues. Transport has to be able to move, not stay plugged into the grid. We cannot place a nuclear reactor on every train, or attach a wind farm to each car. There are many promising avenues for future investigation – improved battery technology, greater use of public transport, new generations of bio fuels or hydrogen cells – but at the moment, we simply do not know the best path forward.

The last problem is innovation. Since the launch of the 747, we have seen no great technological progress in transport, no paradigm shift that would fundamentally affect the way we live. Some may blame this on the random path of progress for technology, steering away from transport into telecoms and computers. Perhaps. But there seem many other technological possibilities such as Personal Rapid Transit or High Speed Rail that we simply have not fully exploited. If the example of space shows us anything, it is that cultural shift can be as powerful as science in driving progress.

Of course, these three problems ultimately all reduce to the same issue. Either we discover a way to change and adapt our current systems, and tackle simultaneously the problems of congestion, climate and stagnation. Or we let things limp on much as they are now, irrevocably sliding towards congestion.

As a society we have a choice we need to make between two strategies to tackle this: the strategy of the Planners or the strategy of Victorians.

At the moment, we seem to be leaning towards the Planners' view: a vast, bureaucratic thirty-year mission to move us away from our cars onto state owned buses and transit.

The threat of global warming, the Planners argue, means we must do all we can to subsidise the development of electric cars and move passengers from the road to public transport. Aviation has become an unaffordable luxury; we must halt its growth and for now focus on optimising what capacity we already have. Railway privatisation was a mistake, but with careful regulation perhaps we can harmonise enough of the current industry structures to make the railway work better. If not, we can always slowly take each franchise as it ends back into public ownership, and rebuild the old British Rail.

We made a mistake back in the 1980s when we followed the Americans, say the Planners, and moved away from planning and central control, but it's not too late. Under one big push, the plan to end all plans, we can simultaneously deal with the dangers of cars and tackle climate change for the bargain. We can bring back co-ordination, control, a more civilised world.

The argument of this book has been that this, our current strategy, won't work.

Planning the future is an unwinnable game. It is possible that the century of the car is over, but – equally – it is possible that its long reign is just beginning. We're still not sure of what the economically appropriate price is to put on carbon, or whether demand for transport is even going up – nobody would want to bet their life that we won't slowly transition away from the automobile in the coming decades.

But then again, the car might come roaring back, more successful than ever, new technologies of electric batteries and computer controlled driving reshaping our transport infrastructure as fundamentally as Henry Ford's production line.

As we have seen, the history of transport is unpredictable. It is next to impossible to plan real innovation, let alone shift the cultural mores and human nature that can so fundamentally affect the way people behave. A grand plan to move us from cars to trains will inevitably cost a fortune, fall behind schedule and probably have next-to-no effect on congestion, carbon emissions or growth.

But there is another way.

Plans are ultimately unavoidable, but we can adopt a cautious, flexible strategy, keeping our options open. We know that our population will increase, so we'll likely need more capacity. Trains and buses will never be able to replace all the current uses of cars, so we'll need to open our infrastructure up to reform in search of new ideas.

By opening up transport to competition and innovation, we'll drive new technology and business models. These new companies will in turn develop new ways to cut carbon emissions, to transport us faster and to decrease congestion.

We can build this agenda upon nothing more the same classical liberal principles that have guided the rest of our economy to growth. New competition should be brought in to explore fresh ideas. Externalities should pay for their costs. Scarce supply should be rationed by price. Political decisions should be taken by those most impacted.

When applied to the realm of transport, a new and coherent programme emerges.

A New Agenda for the UK
So what does all this mean in practice for the UK?

Climate change is a serious, fundamental problem to the modern world – but we should tackle it with a carbon tax, not a lengthy plan. We will almost certainly need a thousand new innovations, fundamentally changing the supply chains and patterns of comparative advantage in the economy. No politician or civil servant can hope to predict this; but they do not need to. All that is needed is the imposition of the tax at the correct level, and then to allow the market to do the work of economic calculation.

In this light, much of the debate over what today's environmental worries mean for the sector becomes much easier to judge. There may be many good reasons for investing in a High Speed 2 railway line – as a key part of business infrastructure, or as part of a strategic attempt to heal the North–South divide – but thinking of it as an environmental measure is mistaken. We should not be attempting to shift passengers from the roads to public transport; instead we should set a fair carbon price and allow individuals to decide their own preference. Trying to limit aviation expansion is costly gesture politics rather than a real environmental measure.

Prices can also help us ration supply. On the roads, an introduction of pricing systems could ease up congestion and help preserve valuable road space at rush hour for those who truly need it. Scarce airport slots at Heathrow could be used by those who most need to fly out of that airport – as long as they pay the going market rate, rather than the artificially low prices they now enjoy.

Regulation is always a second-best solution, relying as it does on imperfect chains of accountability, incentives and information. It should be avoided whenever possible, and replaced with the more honest counterweight of competition. For example, keeping Heathrow regulated is probably doing more harm than good; artificially keeping its prices low and skewing its priorities in favour of retail over transport.

When regulation is unavoidable, however, we should seek to make it as effective as possible through the provision of as much information as is feasible. Monolithic national bodies such as Network Rail should be broken up, to give the Office for Rail Regulation a better idea of what realistic cost efficiencies can and should be. Accountability should be enhanced by devolving decisions over appropriate levels of subsidy as close possible so that the pool of voters in charge matches the pool of users who will benefit.

Whenever possible, we should seek to involve the private sector in the development of the infrastructure that the UK currently lacks. It should be the private sector that takes the lead in new major roads, procurement of train stock and development of airports. To make this easier, it is crucial that we speed up the planning system, rather than allowing crucial infrastructure projects to languish in inquiries for year after year.

The UK is now at a critical moment. Its current capacity is reaching its limits – its roads and airports full, its railway system falling behind the gleaming new High Speed systems in China or on the Continent.

It is for this reason that the current stale arguments over privatisation and climate change are so harmful, and a distraction away from the real challenges we face. We simply won't stop climate change by cancelling a third runway, or rein in costs of the railways by the umpteenth new regulator.

Our only hope in the long term is to unleash the possibilities of new technology and political reform. We need to increase competition, choice and private ownership in our transport systems, so that entrepreneurs can dazzle us with new ideas and possibilities. We need to reform our political, legal and planning systems, to stop red tape getting in the way. We need to make sure that the government doesn't prop up overly large, stagnant private monopolies, pumping them full of public money and stopping the entrance of new companies and new ideas.

Remember the initial mysteries we wondered about: the crowding of our roads, the dire state of our airports, the constantly rising ticket fares. These all are the legacy of the absence of prices, competition and innovation from the transport sector.

We can change things. The dynamic spirit that once made Britain's transport the envy of the world clearly still survives, even if it rests dormant – this is still the country of the engineering expertise of Rolls-Royce; half the world's best F1 teams; of Riversimple and the attempt to re-engineer the car; of Virgin Galactic and the business ventures that may one day take us up to space. Encouraged again, and with the right programme of reforms, we can prove wrong the assumptions that things have to stay as they are.

If we take a couple of sensible steps and enjoy a bit of luck, Gridlock Nation can still be avoided.

GLOSSARY

Agglomeration	Economists have found that people who live and work closer together are more economically productive. These increases in wealth are known as 'agglomeration' effects. See Chapter 3.
Barriers to entry	Some industries are easier to enter than others. Those obstacles that make it difficult to start a company in a new industry are known as 'barriers to entry'. They include large capital requirements, regulatory restrictions and geographical constraints.
CAA	Short for the Civil Aviation Authority. The body in charge of economic and security regulation for the Aviation industry.
Cap and trade	'Cap and trade' is a common shorthand for a proposed policy regime to tackle global warming. It involves auctioning off permits giving the right to emit certain volumes of carbon. There are minor technical differences, but this would have largely equivalent effects to a carbon tax.
Cap-and-collar	The current TOCs are subject to what are known as 'cap-and-collar' price support. Under this agreement, the government agrees to make up for losses that are more than 5 per cent off the company's predictions, but equally confiscates profits that are more than 5 per cent higher. This proposal is designed to make it harder for TOCs to go bust in a general economic recession, but arguably reduces incentives for improvement.

Carbon tax	Economists propose that we should tackle the externalities of carbon with a new tax. By creating a price for carbon emissions, we utilise the power of the market to find the most cost effective means of reducing carbon emissions.
CBA	Short for Cost-Benefit Analysis. See Chapter 6.
Congestion Charge	A charge applied to vehicles entering highly congested areas. This is intended to make drivers pay for the inconvenience they are causing to other users of the road, and consequently make traffic flow more smoothly.
DfT	Short for the Department for Transport.
Electrification	The process of upgrading tracks and infrastructure to allow the running of trains powered by electricity.
Externalities	Economics term for effects, both positive and negative, that are not captured by prices and the market process.
KPI	Short for Key Performance Indicator. Alongside price controls, government regulation and subsidies are often conditional on other targets that must be achieved.
NBR	Short for Net Benefit Ratio. This is the bottom line of Cost-Benefit Analysis, the predicted ratio of a project's benefits to costs. Standard procedure is only to move ahead with a project if this number exceeds two.
Network Rail	Network Rail is the non-profit organisation responsible for owning and maintaining the railway track and stations. It is the successor to the private sector Railtrack, which went bust in the wake of the Hatfield rail accident.
ORR	Short for the Office of Rail Regulation. A body responsible for the safety and economic regulation of the railways.

PFI	Short for Private Finance Initiative. A PFI is a public sector project paid for (and often operated) by the private sector.
PPP	Short for Public Private Partnership.
PRT	Short for Personal Rapid Transit. See Chapter 12.
PTE	Short for Passenger Travel Executive. Local government bodies responsible for public transport in large urban areas.
PV	Short for Present Value. The equivalent current value of any cost, revenue, or stream of such in the future. Calculating Present Values makes it easier to calculate whether to proceed with any particular investment decision.
RAB	Short for Regulatory Asset Base. See Chapter 3.
Railtrack	Railtrack was the private sector organisation responsible for owning and maintaining the railway track and stations. It was succeeded by Network Rail.
ROSCO	Short for Rolling Stock Operating Companies. These companies own the actual trains and carriages, which are then leased out in turn to TOCs.
RPI-X	RPI-X regulation is common shorthand for a particular style of regulation. Under this system, a company is allowed to grow the prices it charges in line with the RPI measure of inflation, minus some factor (the X) of efficiency improvements the regulator expects it to make.
Single till	'Single till' refers to the regulation practice in aviation of limiting not just the profits directly from providing aviation itself, but associated retail revenue.

Smart growth	A planner philosophy that land and transport planning should deliberately aim to create compact, walkable urban centres, reducing sprawl. Also known as a 'compact city'.
SRA	Short for the Strategic Rail Authority. Set up in 2001 by New Labour to provide direction for the railway industry. It was abandoned in 2006, and its functions taken back in-house to the Department for Transport.
Stern Report	An influential 2006 UK government report that aimed to measure the economic costs of climate change. See Chapter 4.
TFL	Short for Transport for London. Responsible for co-ordinating public transport in London.
TOC	Short for Train Operating Company. These are the companies that win franchise bids for a section of the network, and directly provide passenger services. It includes such companies as First Great Western and Virgin Trains.
VPF	Short for Value per Passenger Fatality. See Chapter 7.

BIBLIOGRAPHY

Manuscripts

Coates, W. H. (1942, July). Report on The Transport Problem in Great Britain. TNA MT 64/9.

Letter from A. T. V. Robinson to the Minister for Transport (Sir John Reith). (1940, May 29). TNA MT64/10.

Letter from Barbara Castle to John Diamond. (1967, September 7). TNA T319/1052.

Letter from I. H. Lightman to Vinter. (1967, August 11). TNA T319/1052.

Letter from R. C. W. Cox to Downey. (1967, December 6). TNA T319/1052.

McKean, D. (1969, July). Toll Roads – Minutes of 21 July. TNA T319/1052.

Reports

Bowerman, A. (2007). *The Costs and Benefits of Road Pricing: Comparing Nationwide Charging with Project-Based Schemes*. London: IEA.

Boyfield, K. (2003). *A Market in Airport Slots*. London: Institute of Economic Affairs.

Boyfield, K. (1994). *Plane Commonsense: The case for feeder-reliever airports in the South East*. London: Adam Smith Institute.

Crozier, P. (2001). *Why British Rail Privatization has failed*. London.

Department for Transport. (2011). *Developing a sustainable framework for UK aviation: Scoping document*.

Duranton, G. (2009). The Fundamental Law of Road Congestion: Evidence from US cities. *NBER Working Paper* .

(February 2011). *Economic Case for HS2.* Department for Transport.

Helm, D. (2009). *Utility regulation, the RAB and the cost of capital.* Oxford.

Helm, D., Wardlaw, J., & Caldecott, B. (2009). *Delivering a 21st Century Infrastructure for Britain.* Policy Exchange.

(February 2011). *High Speed Rail: Investing in Britain's Future Consultation.* Department for Transport.

(2010). *International cost efficiency benchmarking of Network Rail.* Office of Rail Regulation.

Krugman, P. (2009). *The Increasing Returns Revolution in Trade and Geography.* American Economic Review.

Leunig, T. (2010). *What to do about trains in Britain.* London: Policy Exchange.

Lewis, M. J. (2001). Railways in the Greek and Roman World. In A. /. Guy, *Early Railways. A Selection of Papers from the First International Early Railways Conference* (pp. 8–19).

Martin, I. (2005). *No Way to Run a Railway.* London: Adam Smith Institute.

Millard-Ball, A., & Schipper, L. (2010). *Are we reaching Peak Travel? Trends in Passenger Transport in Industrialized Countries.*

Oakervee OBE FRENG, D. E. (2009). *Thames Estuary Airport Feasibility Review.*

Prud'homme, R. a. (2004). The London congestion charge: a tentative economic appraisal. *Transport Policy .*

Rail Value for Money: Scoping Study Report. (2010).

Road Pricing. (2010). London: Institute for Mechanical Engineers.

Rosewell, B. (2010). *Planning Curses: How to deliver long-term investment in infrastructure.* London: Policy Exchange.

Schafer, A. a. (2000). The future mobility of the world population. *Transportation Research Part A: Policy and Practice .*

Simms, A. (2011). *The New Home Front.*

The Economic Impact of Hub Airports. (2009). London: British Chambers of Commerce.

The Future of Air Transport White Paper. (2003). London: Department for Transport.

The Railways, the Market and the Government. (2006). London: Institute of Economic Affairs.

Treasury, H. (2006). *Stern Review: The Economics of Climate Change.*

Wellings, R., & Lipson, B. (2008). *Towards better transport.* London: Policy Exchange.

Books

Adams, J. (2010). Managing transport risks: what works? In *Risk Theory Handbook.*

Bagwell, P., & Lyth, P. (2002). *Transport in Britain: From Canal Lock to Gridlock.* London: Hambledon and London.

Clark, G. (2007). *A Farewell to Alms.* Princeton University Press.

Glaesar, E. (2011). *Triumph of the City.* Penguin.

Glaister, S., Burnham, J., Stevens, H., & Travers, T. (2006). *Transport Policy in Britain.* Houndmills: Palgrave Macmillan.

Hamilton-Paterson, J. (2010). *Empire of the Clouds: When Britain's Aircraft Ruled the World.* London: Faber and Faber.

Helm, D., & Holt, D. (. (2003). *Air Transport and Infrastructure: The Challenges Ahead.* Oxford: Oxera.

O'Toole, R. (2009). *Gridlock.* Washington D.C.: Cato Institute.

Ridley, M. (2010). *The Rational Optimist.* London: Fourth Estate.

Sampson, A. (1984). *Empires of the Sky: The Politics, Contests and Cartels of World Airlines.* London: Hodder and Stoughton.

Vanderbilt, T. (2008). *Traffic: Why We Drive the Way We Do (and What It Says About Us)*. New York: Allen Lane.

Winston, C. (2010). *Last Exit : Privatization and Deregulation of the U.S. Transportation System*. Brookings Institute Press.

Wolmar, C. (2009). *Blood, Iron and Gold: How the Railways Transformed the World*. London: Atlantic Books.

Wolmar, C. (2002). *Down the Tube: The Battle for London's Underground*. London: Aurum Press.

Wolmar, C. (2007). *Fire and Steam: How the Railways Transformed Britain*. London: Atlantic Books.

Wolmar, C. (2005). *On the Wrong Line: How Ideology and Incompetence Wrecked Britain's Railways*. London: Aurum Press.

Wolmar, C. (2004). *The Subterranean Railway*. London: Atlantic Books.

Worstall, T. (2010). *Chasing Rainbows: How the Green Agenda Defeats Its Aims*. London: Stacey International.

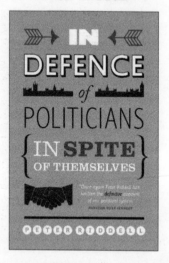

Also available from Biteback

WHICH WAY'S UP?
Nicholas Boles

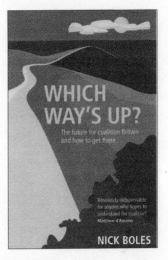

"Absolutely indispensable for anyone who hopes to understand what the coalition is and – more strikingly – what it might be." Matthew D'ancona, *Evening Standard*

In *Which Way's Up?* a leading Conservative moderniser looks at how David Cameron, at the head of a modern coalition government, can transform Britain. This is a wide-ranging examination of the problems (and solutions) facing Britain, from one of the new government's preeminent movers and shakers, as well as a unique chronicle of the first six months of this historic new government.

144pp paperback, £8.99

**Available from all good bookshops or order from
www.bitebackpublishing.com**